e
German
Shepherd Dog
Handbook

Dr. Mary Belle Brazil-Adelman

BARRON'S

Acknowledgements

The American breed standard is reprinted courtesy of the American Kennel Club.

A Word About Pronouns

Many dog lovers feel that the pronoun "it" is not appropriate when referring to a pet that can be such a wonderful part of our lives. For this reason the German Shepherd Dog in this book is referred to as "he" unless the topic specifically relates to female dogs. This by no means implies any preference, nor should it be taken as an indication that either sex is particularly problematic.

Cover Photos

Front cover: Cheryl A. Ertelt (left), Shutterstock (top and bottom right); back cover: Cheryl A. Ertelt; spine: Shutterstock; inside front cover: Cheryl A. Ertelt; inside back cover: Shutterstock.

Text © copyright 2010, 2000 by Mary Belle Brazil-Adelman.

All rights reserved.
No part of this publication may be reproduced or distributed in any form or by any means without the written permission of the copyright owner.

All inquiries should be addressed to:
Barron's Educational Series, Inc.
250 Wireless Boulevard
Hauppauge, New York 11788
www.barronseduc.com

ISBN-13: 978-0-7641-4333-5
ISBN-10: 0-7641-4333-6

Library of Congress Catalog Card No. 2009043184

Library of Congress Cataloging-in-Publication Data
Brazil-Adelman, Mary Belle.
  The German shepherd handbook / Mary Belle Brazil-Adelman.
    p. cm.
  Includes bibliographical references (p.) and index.
  ISBN-13: 978-0-7641-4333-5
  ISBN-10: 0-7641-4333-6
  1. German shepherd dog. I. Title.

SF429.G37 B73 2010
636.737—d 22   2009043184

Printed in China
9 8 7 6 5 4 3 2 1

About the Author

Dr. Mary Belle Brazil-Adelman has a Ph.D. from the University of Illinois at Carbondale. She also has graduate psychology and education degrees from the University of Arkansas. Attaining all of the components (U.D., Chs, H.X., T.D., Sch III, FH, Herding titles, agility and rally titles, training police dogs, and judging), as well as garnering over 175 titles and degrees on five breeds in two countries plus enough showing and judging to become a conformation, herding, tracking, obedience, and Schutzhund judge, has put her in the position to see what the dog needs to know and how to get there efficiently, humanely, and still have some fun in the process. From this research and background, she developed the Optimum Placement Technique (OPT). While servicing a large population that loves its dogs but must have them under control, the first six lessons of the OPT still give all students the tools to develop any potential conformation or performance prospect.

Dr. Brazil-Adelman has served on the board and committees of two national breed clubs, as various officers in many local clubs, and as training director of several clubs, always trying to make contributions that would benefit both people and dogs. She is currently an active club member, trainer, breeder, and exhibitor.

Photo Credits

Mary Belle Brazil-Adelman: pages 41, 87, 122, 143 (left and right); Norvia Behling: pages 20, 29, 30, 36, 46, 54; Kent Dannen: pages xii, 53, 65, 71, 72, 73, 76, 86, 87, 91, 101, 103, 104, 111, 126, 146; Tara Darling: pages 12, 66, 99, 105, 120 (top and bottom), 130, 142, 144, 147; Cheryl A. Ertelt: pages viii, xi, 9, 45, 56, 59, 83, 85, 93, 117, 119, 127, 137, 149, 135; Paulette Johnson: page vi, 3, 49, 98; Pets by Paulette: pages 14, 19, 25, 39, 50, 58, 60, 63, 78, 124, 128; Shutterstock: pages 4, 6, 66, 118; Connie Summers/Paulette Johnson: pages 13, 18, 23, 26, 96; Barb Young/Paulette Johnson: page 83.

Important Note

This book tells the reader how to buy and care for a German Shepherd Dog. The author and publisher consider it important to point out that the advice given in this book is meant primarily for normally developed puppies from a good breeder—that is, dogs of excellent physical health and good character.

Caution is advised in the association of children with dogs, in meeting with other dogs, and in exercising the dog without a leash.

Even well-behaved and carefully supervised dogs sometimes do damage to someone else's property or cause accidents. It is, therefore, in the owner's interest to be adequately insured against such eventualities, and we strongly urge all dog owners to purchase liability policies that cover their dogs.

Contents

Preface

There is no way to list all of the friends, teachers, trainers, and others who have provided information, support, direction, and friendship along the way. They are all special and I thank them. Also, to the editors who had faith in me, to Mordecai Siegal who gave me good advice, and to my agent who helped arrange all the details, a sincere note of appreciation.

I do have to give a special thank you to Dr. Robert Salley, D.V.M. for proofing the chapters dealing with the medical aspects of the book. I also want to thank all the crew at Westside Veterinary Service L.L.P., including Dr. Noel Thomas, D.V.M., A.B.V.P., A.C.T., all the other dedicated veterinarians, as well as Kim Hart and Beverly Colson, and the rest of the office crew. They have so patiently put up with me calling for information, checking spelling, and just lending an ear when needed. You can't train a sick dog very well. They keep the crew at Glendhenmere up and running.

While I took many of the pictures, a variety of others also contributed many photographs to this book, and I appreciate all their efforts.

Special thanks go to all of the editors and evaluators whose comments and suggestions have been sincerely appreciated.

I also want to thank my enduring husband Frank. He has put up with hundreds of friends, trainers, exhibitors, dogs, and all that goes into showing, breeding, and training over the years. I love him dearly and he must love me to still be here and smiling.

For the 2nd edition, all the above still holds true but I want to add a thank you to Kim Broster, Vet tec and nutritional advisor, and Dr. Kirby DVM for helping with the revising of the chapter on Nutrition and Health. Also, I want to give a special thanks to my writing buddy Erika Tracy for help with proofing and encouragement to keep me working. Special thanks to the editor at Barron's for letting me add other photos to illustrate some of the unique exercises of the OPT training program. In spite of what I considered my fantastic descriptions, readers over the past few years have requested photos for clarification.

I want to give special thanks to all of the people who took the time to let

me know how much they enjoyed and appreciated the humane and efficient way-of-life training detailed in the book. I was especially impressed with the number of readers who found this book to be extremely useful in training a wide variety of other breeds.

I hope everyone continues to enjoy this easy communication system for training dogs and continues to send me comments and suggestions. This is a truly wonderful breed and will reward your kindness and attention with love and companionship for years to come.

Dr. Mary Belle Brazil-Adelman
Master Trainer
Glendhenmere Kennels

Introduction

Every book should have a beginning. I thought a long time before I came up with one that I thought would help the reader to see the material from my perspective. Since the OPT (Optimum Placement Technique © 1980) is so radically different from any other training system I have reviewed, I think this is necessary for you to understand where I came from and where I wanted to go. I will say part of my journey is still a work in progress, but I feel I have come a long way toward the goals I set in the beginning. I hope this book will help you establish your goals and reach them as you and your dog develop increasingly better skills in both mental and physical communication.

I arrived on the AKC obedience scene in 1973 after having been given a German Shepherd Dog. I was told Beowulf was purebred but time and experience have made me wonder. He was, however, the greatest dog in the world at the time for both me and my family. He was a born alpha male with, I am sure, at least some demon involved. By the time he was six months old, he had effectively terrorized the entire neighborhood and almost cost us our garbage collection services.

A neighbor who had a son the same age as mine and also a very large unmanageable dog called one day to suggest we attend an obedience class with our dogs. It sounded like a good idea at the time. After one week, her dog ran away and never returned. My dog felt that he had been granted a vacation in paradise. He suddenly had been given a large basketball gym full of people and dogs he could intimidate and terrorize. I spent the entire ten-week class on one end of the gym while the rest of the class worked on the other.

I was introduced to chain collars, force training, and frustration. I had trained dogs all my life to do whatever I wanted them to do. I even had a horse I trained to come when called, lie down, bow, dance, and retrieve. She also could untie a handkerchief off any of her feet. I did it all with a cotton halter, a few feet of cotton rope, and lots of corn. I couldn't understand the jerking, pushing, and yelling at the dog that seemed to be the accepted method of obedience training.

We moved shortly after that class and I joined another class at the new place. In the new ten-week class I was exposed to prong collars, shock collars, and the ear pinch for retrieving. The prong collar produced no results. Beowulf's pain threshold was so high, he couldn't even feel the shock collar set on the highest setting. He was indifferent to the ear pinch. I started training by my old methods and was moderately successful. I continued working several feet from all the other students. Beowulf was still very aggressive to both people and other dogs.

Shortly thereafter I acquired an Australian Cattle Dog. If you haven't tried to obedience train one of these, you really have missed an exciting experience. They have a higher pain threshold than the GSD and very little genetic desire to do obedience. They also fall apart quickly in obedience training when you correct them. They have an exceedingly high pain threshold, but the corrections frustrate and upset them.

I asked the instructor why they trained the way they did since I was having such poor results. I also mentioned about my earlier experiences with my dogs and the trick horse using food and no force. I was informed that this was the way dogs were trained and that I obviously didn't know anything. That sounded like a challenge to me.

So, I set about learning about the world of dog training and competition. It was a long road, but it has been one of the most exciting and rewarding experiences of my life. In the course of my research, developing my own training methods, and training dogs of all breeds, I have titled dogs to the top levels in several fields including, but not limited to, the CH, UD, RE, HX, WTCH, TD, Sch III, FH, and agility. I have trained police dogs, search and rescue dogs, stage acting dogs, therapy dogs, and have achieved many other accomplishments in the canine world. I have instructed in seminars from coast to coast and sold my books and videos around the world. But my greatest gift to the canines and their handlers has been the OPT program of communication versus subjugation in the world of training. I cannot stress how great it was to have started with one extremely difficult breed and two with excessively high pain thresholds. If they had been the genetically and physically suitable breeds of dogs trainable by these early training methods, I probably would never have challenged them.

Since putting a CDX on both of those dogs after being told by several obedience instructors and many friends it would never happen, I have developed a very stoic attitude toward criticism. Only recently I was told I would never put a Herding started title on my eight-year-old Australian Cattle Dog. I got the Herding started one year later and was able to put 37 on her including the HX (Herding Excellent) and WTCH (Working Trial Champion) before she died just after turning 14 years of age.

Somewhere along the way, I picked up a Ph.D. in education with several degrees in psychology. I love researching in education and developing new ways of communicating with both people and animals.

Also on my journey to learn, I was on the board of a national breed club and chaired the first herding committee and event for another national. I felt that learning as much as I could would help me develop the OPT and expand my resources and skills. Eventually I was granted an AKC license to judge Conformation and Herding as well as a provisional license to judge obedience and tracking. In the 80s, I was a member of the board of one of the largest Schutzhund clubs in America and became a Schutzhund judge, judging the Schutzhund trial for the Doberman national.

Therefore, I feel that I am now in a position to say I understand dogs and the world of canine competition sufficiently to bring you materials that will help you develop greater communication skills with your dog regardless of your eventual goals. At this point, I feel that I really do understand not only the game of showing, but also the real world of living with these wonderful animals on a day-to-day basis. Many of these training methods are similar to the techniques I used when teaching students in 1st through 12th grades in school, college-level courses, and as a guidance counselor and career educator. My emphasis on communication rather than punishment allowed me a wide range of success in schools that were often considered challenging. Many of my obedience students have remarked that they acquired teaching tools that were extremely effective in their daily lives both as parents and schoolteachers.

I truly believe that if the world treated the animals and each other with this type of patience and understanding, we would all live a happier and more rewarding life.

I hope you enjoy this book as much as I enjoyed writing it. I would appreciate any comments or feedback you may wish to contribute.

Good Luck and Happy Heeling.

Dr. Mary Belle Brazil-Adelman
E-mail: maryba@toast.net
www.Glendhenmere.com

Chapter One

Overview of the German Shepherd Dog

Versatility of the Breed

Among German Shepherd Dog fanciers there is a quote, "There are two kinds of dogs: those who are German Shepherds and all those others who wish they were." The variation on this theme is "There are two kinds of dog owners: those who own German Shepherd Dogs and those who don't know what they're missing." These probably express rather biased views, but they do honestly reflect the feelings of those of us who have had the experience of owning one or more outstanding members of this most versatile and rewarding of all dog breeds.

While all purebreds have been designed to meet specific needs of their humans over the centuries, none has been engineered with such a deep and varied overall capacity for work, play, companionship, love, loyalty, and endurance and presented in such an excitingly elegant, yet durable, package as the German Shepherd Dog. It is the only dog

designed to execute the ground-covering, breathtaking flying-trot that is one of the hallmarks of the breed. Only bad breeding practices and the handler's inability to provide correct training can limit this remarkable animal's capacity for performance and service. There may be individual tasks that other breeds can perform better, but no other single breed has ever surpassed the German Shepherd Dog in mastering such a wide range of skills.

Even those specimens that are handicapped through poor breeding selection, improper nutrition, and faulty socialization often still retain sufficient genetic material to make good home companions and adequate protection dogs. These animals are often handicapped, however, by bodies that fail to respond to the stout hearts and ready minds that are their legacy. They are tragic evidence of breeders whose greed and ignorance result in the mixing of inappropriate gene pools.

When all the rules are followed and the proper gene mix is achieved, this is a breed capable of attaining almost any goal possible with a canine. Each of these talents, and the skills needed to develop them, will be covered later in detail. This is simply a rapid overview of some of this breed's remarkable abilities.

Obedience

German Shepherd Dogs are excellent obedience dogs, easy to train with food and praise. They can work for extended periods of time and accomplish as much as their handler is capable of teaching them. They also make ideal agility dogs. Their keen sense of timing and concentration on taking directions are key factors in successful agility work.

Conformation

Conformation or breed showing allows the owner to display exceptional representations of what the German Shepherd Dog should look like both standing and in motion. Of all dogs shown, this is the most unique breed in presentation. Most breeds are poised or stacked with all four legs set almost like a table. Sometimes the back legs are positioned slightly behind the dog, but always even with each other. German Shepherd Dogs, however, are stacked with the rear leg near the handler positioned so the foot is almost directly in line with the navel and slightly to the outside of the dog's body. The leg closest to the judge is pulled back until the hock is perpendicular to the ground to emphasize the smoothly sloping topline and the correct turn of stifle.

When gaited, if structurally correct, they really are poetry in motion.

Herding

In Germany, this breed was originally developed as a versatile herding dog. Today they are still widely used for working sheep and other types of stock. The rising sport of herding has brought this exceptionally skilled breed more into the spotlight. They can be trained for all competition courses and, while most skilled with sheep, can handle a wide variety of other stock.

Companion Dogs

As a breed, they excel in their willingness to help their human companions. To the blind, they have offered freedom of movement undreamed of prior to the Seeing Eye program. They have provided a way to enter the mainstream lifestyle that has been closed for centuries to the visually impaired.

Only recently has their capacity for learning and helping been extended to the hearing and physically impaired. Current programs certify both hearing and assistance dogs, helping them to enjoy the same hard-won privileges afforded to the Seeing Eye dogs. Therapy dogs are often used to help cheer those people confined to institutions where pets are no longer available to them. However, there are also newer levels of dogs working with a variety of emotionally impaired children and adults. The empathic level exhibited by a German Shepherd Dog is almost uncanny and only time and research will reveal the extent to which they can be of help to medically, mentally, and physically impaired people of all ages.

Rescue Dogs

Many outstanding rescue stories abound to attest to the tracking and scenting talents of this breed. Aside from their use as tracking competition dogs, they are used most frequently to find lost people in all types of weather and under a great variety of conditions. Neither snow, water, nor debris can prevent their detection of bodies both living and dead. In remote and almost inaccessible areas, they have been parachuted down from both planes and helicopters with their handlers to conduct searches for lost or snow-buried victims. They have even been trained to ride a chair lift in snow country.

Protection Dogs

The German Shepherd Dog is an outstanding Schutzhund dog. Literally translated, Schutzhund means "protection dog." Part of the Schutzhund competition includes the demonstration of tracking skills. Schutzhund also demands extensive obedience and the demonstration of protection skills. It is a very popular sport in Europe and enjoys growing success in America.

Police Dogs

Schutzhund as a sport should not be confused with the working police dogs. The skills, while similar, are in practice vastly different. However, the German Shepherd Dog is skilled in

both areas and can switch from sport to work with ease and speed, thus making it one of the most popular breeds in the world for police work.

The German Shepherd Dog is known worldwide for his drug-finding abilities. It is also outstanding in finding a wide variety of arson-causing agents as well as a number of explosive ingredients. These skills enable law enforcers to discover the sources of fires and detect bombs before they cause damage.

Their keen scenting abilities make them valuable for such esoteric types of work as detecting leaks in gas pipe lines, finding Gypsy moth eggs, and exposing contraband items such as fruit, exotic animals, and other objects with various types of scent patterns.

War Dogs

They have been used extensively in every war since their development as danger detectors, attack dogs, sentry dogs, ambulance dogs to locate wounded or dead soldiers,

messenger dogs, and as companions and aids in many ways to the soldiers with whom they serve. They have rescued crews of downed planes, worked on patrols (they have been known to detect a human up to 150 yards away), detected mines buried several feet underground, and, on occasion, have even been trained to parachute from airplanes. They have a remarkable ability to discriminate between the living and the dead when time is an essential element in the search for wounded soldiers.

During World War I, and in all subsequent military encounters, the German Shepherd Dog distinguished itself as a useful and efficient member of the military. Due to its outstanding performance and versatility during World War II, the German Shepherd Dog was declared the official dog of the United States Armed Forces.

Entertaining Dogs

Though many were brought back to the United States after the various wars, the greatest impact of German Shepherd Dogs on the general public has been most widely spread through movies and television. The charismatic appeal of such stars as Rin Tin Tin and Strongheart brought this breed into the hearts of many Americans. This is a breed that lends itself to heroic stories and brave deeds.

The German Shepherd Dog has something to offer any owner looking for a companion, helper, guardian, or beautiful friend. It is a breed apart. If you don't believe me, just try one.

Chapter Two

History of the Breed

Development of the Breed

Max von Stephanitz's dream was to breed the most versatile of all working-herding dogs. He wanted a dog that would guard the flocks as well as the shepherd's family. One that could be gentle with children and nonthreatening to strangers, yet severe and swift to punish those who might wish to do harm. He envisioned a dog that could cover great distances in pursuit of duty, yet lie patiently beside the owner until needed. His goal was to produce a faithful friend and an efficient herding dog that would know no equal in the world.

The rugged cavalry captain Max von Stephanitz was hardly what one could call a romantic, but the pursuit of his dream led him to visit many wild and remote countries and consumed a major portion of his life. His writings and the results of his extensive breeding program have left us a legacy that contains all of the romance and adventure one could ever hope for. The creation of the German Shepherd Dog is truly one of the most exciting and rewarding stories in the history of the domestic dog.

Almost the first 300 pages of von Stephanitz's *The German Shepherd Dog in Word and Picture* are devoted to a detailed accounting of the major portion of all of the existing herding breeds that were working anywhere in the world at that time. This tome of more than 900 pages, written by the dedicated researcher and breeder, stands as one of the most extensive books ever written on the breeding, structure, training, and history of any breed. Von Stephanitz was a perfectionist who knew what he wanted, worked his way through much of the available genetic material, and then worked persistently to combine and recombine those elements in such a manner as to produce the closest living example of his inner visual picture of perfection.

For his base stock, he went to the finest kennels that were producing dogs that had some of the requirements he demanded. He mixed various herding dogs until he found those that were closest to what he envisioned and that could produce progeny that displayed the most valued characteristics. He was ruthless in his selection and rejection process, always keeping the picture of the final product before him. He sought

and found quality dogs that carried the *Hauptpreishuetenfuer Herdengebrauchshunde* (HGH) or herding dog degree. The HGH is earned in the field under competition much as the Schutzhund, obedience, tracking, or police dog degrees. Above all, he sought a quality of greatness in a dog just a little more willing to give, just a fraction more devoted, and with a certain look of character and nobility.

Early Breeding

The early breeding aim set by the German Shepherd Dog Club of Germany (*Verein fur Deutsche Schaferhunde* or SV) called for a highly gifted and efficient dog with a perfect body build. The SV has become the largest individual breed club in the world and, under the early guidance of its founding president, Cap-

tain Max von Stephanitz, is credited with the establishment of the German Shepherd Dog as a specific breed. Von Stephanitz frequently stressed the fact that shepherd dog breeding was the breeding of working dogs; otherwise it would no longer be shepherd dog breeding at all. He insisted on the training of at least all those dogs that were destined to be used for breeding, and that the point should be made to avoid kennel keeping and mass-production of the shepherd dog. He defined those dogs that were "worthwhile" as breeding stock and indicated that they should be so selected, not on the basis of their moneymaking potential, but on their future contribution to the breed.

His essential vision projected a dog with great working ability, loyal, highly trainable, and with an incorruptible character. "Do right and fear no one" was his watchword, and while body conformation was important, one of the basic tenets in the guidelines of the breed was and remains, "Utility is the true criterion of beauty."

While herding was the original focal point of the breed, von Stephanitz recognized the evolving needs of the twentieth century. Herding no longer dominated the scene and industrialization, urbanization, and expanding populations made increasing demands on the world of the German Shepherd Dog. By World War I, German Shepherd Dogs were available to perform such services as sentry and patrol, search and rescue, and message carrier on far-flung battlefields while still maintaining their popularity with many companion dog owners.

Importation to the United States

In 1906, a bitch (female dog) named Mira v. Offingen was the first German Shepherd Dog to be imported to the United States. She was shown several times before being returned to Germany by her owner, Otto Gross. Queen of Switzerland, owned by Adolph Vogt, was the first German Shepherd Dog to be officially registered by the American Kennel Club. In 1913, the first two champion German Shepherd Dogs were registered.

The breed experienced slow growth during World War I due to the extreme anti-German sentiment in the United States. The American Kennel Club, in an effort to quell the negative emotions, officially changed the breed from "German Sheepdogs," as they were currently registered, to "Shepherd Dogs." This did little to help the breed at that time.

At the end of World War I following the Armistice in 1918, many soldiers, impressed with the German Shepherd Dog's unique style and ability, returned home with dogs they had acquired in Europe. The stories they told of the bravery, intelligence, and dedication exhibited by this breed revived the flagging interest of the American public. Sparked by these stories, silent film directors jumped to give the public two new heroes: Rin Tin Tin and Strongheart.

Rin Tin Tin

Lee Duncan, a returning soldier, brought the original Rin Tin Tin puppy from France. Born in 1919 from parents that were probably war dogs, he lived to be 13 years of age. As with today's Lassie, several generations of German Shepherd Dogs named Rin Tin Tin carried on both the name and the legacy.

Strongheart

Strongheart, born in Germany in 1917, was a fully trained German police dog. His real name was Etzel von Oeringen and he was brought to America by Bruno Hoffman, owned by actress-writer Jane Murfin, and trained for the movies by Larry Trimble.

These two dogs probably had the most influence in promoting this breed in America, as everyone wanted to own a marvelous dog just like them. The dark years of WWI were swept away by the charisma and glitter of these two heroic silent screen icons.

German Shepherd Dogs were imported regularly to build the rapidly growing demand for these dogs. In the 1920s, the first solid black German Shepherd Dog was shown and finished as Ch Freia of Humboldtpark owned by Mr. Widener.

Breeders, exhibitors, and the general public found these dogs to be desirable for their beauty and utility. However, for a period of time, the German connection tended to produce negative feelings in a number of people due to the impact of the war. For a while in England the breed was called Alsatians or Alsatian Wolf Dogs, though it is doubtful that any wolf has been used for development of the breed for hundreds of years. In 1977, the name German Shepherd Dog was officially given to the breed and remains as such throughout most of the world.

The German Shepherd Dog Club of America was founded in 1913 by 26 founding members. This group merged with the Shepherd Dog Club of New England, which published the first issue of *The Shepherd Dog Review* in 1924. Today there are over 3,000 members both in America and abroad.

In the late 1920s, several German Siegers were imported to America to be bred with the progeny of Mira. These became the foundation for the German Shepherd Dog breed in America. However, a strong infusion of imports continued throughout the early years, keeping both the American and German dogs of a similar type or look.

Recent History of German Shepherd Dogs in the United States

Toward the end of the 1960s, the breed in America began a slow evolution toward a slightly lower-stationed dog with more depth of chest and turn of stifle. This trend has continued on into the present, producing some dogs of elegant grace and fluid motion that are simply breathtaking when in motion. Unfortunately, a few breeders have gone to extremes, producing some dogs with exaggerated slope to the topline that has resulted in dogs that are unable to move efficiently. On the other end of the breeding scale are the breeders that lack a clear picture of what a German Shepherd Dog should be and therefore resort to the simple, but often disastrous, option of simply breeding two registered dogs together and hoping for the best.

The 1970s and 80s were periods of extreme transitions in both Germany and America. The German dogs were shortened and made slightly stockier. They developed, in many cases, backs that roached. In America, the "overangulated" dog gained much favor in dog shows. This dog was inefficient in working and,

because it was bred for looks alone, was often lacking in both character and ability. At the same time, the general public was getting more involved in random breeding as well as importing dogs that often did not complement the American gene pool.

Bad breeding, importing, selling dogs that were too aggressive for the average person to handle, and allowing dogs to grow up untrained and unruly caused many to lose interest in the breed. This marked a turning point in the breed.

The 1990s saw serious breeders looking more to the all-purpose dog that was described in the original standard. Obedience and tracking have often been achieved by top-ranking breed stock and a few have managed to acquire the Schutzhund title. But for the most part, the dogs had few performance titles and even fewer health-related certifications. This is rapidly changing. Today, many of the top show dogs, destined to become the bloodstock of the breed, are sporting not only the designation of "champion," but also a great variety of performance titles and health certifications.

DNA Testing

Another major step toward slowing down profiteering breeders who often use dogs with false papers or breed dogs with little or no merit is the instigation of the DNA-testing program (identifying individual dogs through their gene patterns). For years there was a vague assumption that everyone was honestly representing the dogs that were being bred, especially show breeding. This was proven to be an invalid assumption when DNA was used to determine that certain progeny were not, in fact, out of the dogs as stated on their papers. This shook up the dog world and encouraged many conscientious breeders to have their dogs DNA tested and registered with the AKC. DNA registration should go a long way in the next decade to help improve all of the breeds.

Along with DNA registration comes expanding research into DNA markers for many inherited problems. If correctly used, this advancement should see a marked improvement in the overall health of many breeds, including the German Shepherd Dog.

Herding Titles

With the advent of herding added to the AKC performance agenda, breeders were able to more conveniently test for herding instinct. Many champions started to sport herding titles along with obedience, tracking, agility, and other performance titles. The addition of the Working Dog program to the AKC's performance venue should go a long way toward encouraging breeders to validate their breed stock's working abilities.

Space would not permit the listing of all the dogs with championships and titles but many American kennels have produced an abundance of both. One need only flip through the pages of *The German Shepherd Dog Review* (the official magazine of the German Shepherd Dog Club of America) to be constantly exposed to the future greatness of this breed.

You will see top dogs from both America and Germany, dogs of excellence in many diverse areas, and articles on a wide variety of topics written by leading authorities. *The German Shepherd Quarterly* is an independently published magazine that contains examples of both American and German dogs. It also features, in great length and with pictures, the kennels that have and still are producing the top breeding stock in this breed. Most issues cover, in depth, at least one outstanding sire or dam. There is often an interview with the owner(s) of an established and recognized kennel.

Check the Appendix for the listing of books on the breed and addresses of German Shepherd–related clubs as well as e-mail addresses leading to AKC, German Shepherd Dogs, and other related areas.

Any breed tends to lose its unique look and characteristics if each generation of dog breeder does not specifically select to breed only the best. Today, the range of dogs bearing German Shepherd Dog registration papers varies from excellent representations to dogs that bear little or no resemblance to the breed. Only the future will reveal what the German Shepherd Dog will become, but today is where the challenge lies. Education that produces breeders who will use all of the available resources, who will keep a keen eye on breed type and skills, and who will have the integrity to do the right thing is the key to the future continued success of this wonderful breed.

Chapter Three

The Standard
and the Pedigree

The Standard

Breed standards are very specific in some points and rather vague or general in others to allow for some variability within the breed. The German Shepherd Dog started with a standard from Germany accepted by the SV (the German Shepherd Dog Club of Germany). This standard came with the breed to America and was originally accepted by the German Shepherd Dog Club of America (GSDCA). Through the years it has been expanded and elaborated to cover in more detail those aspects of the breed that Americans felt needed to be addressed by both judges and breeders. Even so, there have been only a few changes in the standard over the years due to the involved process this requires.

The complete American (AKC) standard (as approved and submitted by the German Shepherd Dog Club of America) is available online or by writing to the GSDCA. The AKC sells a video endorsed by the German Shepherd Dog Club of America. This video takes the breed standard by section and both describes it and shows dogs representing the area under discussion. It is informative and a useful tool in the identification and selection process.

Description

The standard calls for a dog that is, on first impression, strong, agile, well muscled, alert, and full of life. The dog should be longer than tall, deep bodied, and present an outline of smooth curves rather than angles. In looks it should be substantial and not spindly, giving the impression, both at rest and in motion, of muscular fitness and nimbleness without any look of clumsiness or soft living. The ideal dog is stamped with a look of quality and nobility—difficult to define, but unmistakable when present. Often referred to as the look of eagles, it is a quality that separates the truly great German Shepherd Dogs from all others and in dogs, as in people, it really is impossible to describe, but equally impossible to miss when present.

The dog should be aloof, but approachable, quietly standing his ground, showing confidence and willingness to meet overtures without himself making them.

Bitches (females) should be between 22 and 24 inches (listed as 55 cm and 60 cm in the German Standard) and dogs (males) between 24 and 26 inches (same as 60 to 65 cm). The difference in using centimeters instead of inches (people reading cm to equal inches) may account for some misinformed feeling that German-born dogs are somehow much bigger than American dogs. They may be, but the standard for size is identical in both countries. Throughout this book, except when specifically indicated, the generic term "dog" shall include both males and females but be referred to in the masculine form.

The German Shepherd Dog should have a body that is longer than tall with a desirable ratio of 10 to 8.5. The head is noble, cleanly chiseled, strong without coarseness, not fine, and in proportion to the body. There must be a keen and intelligent expression. There should be no confusion in determining the distinctly masculine male from the obviously feminine bitch German Shepherd Dog.

The topline is not parallel to the ground as the withers should be higher than and sloping into a level back. (This, however, would not present a level topline in motion, a fact that is very confusing if you do not understand the difference between the back and the total topline.) The FCI (International Association of Dog Clubs) gives

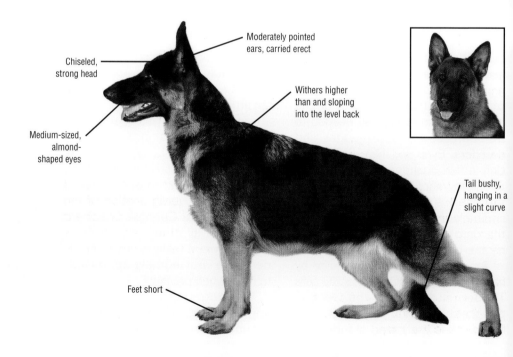

Chiseled, strong head

Moderately pointed ears, carried erect

Medium-sized, almond-shaped eyes

Withers higher than and sloping into the level back

Tail bushy, hanging in a slight curve

Feet short

a very nice description stating that the upper line runs, without any visible break, from the set-on of the neck over the well-defined withers and over the back very slightly sloping to the horizontal line, onto the gradually slanting rump. This straight, strongly developed back without sag or roach that is relatively short pretty well describes most AKC Champion (Ch) German Shepherd Dogs.

The tail should extend at least to the hock joint and should set smoothly into the croup, low rather than high. At rest the tail should hang in a slight curve like a saber.

The German Shepherd Dog should have a double coat of medium length. The outer coat should be as dense as possible, hair straight, harsh, and lying close to the body.

Colors

The German Shepherd Dog varies in color, and most colors are permissible with a preference toward strong rich colors. Solid white German Shepherds are disqualified from competition in conformation; however, they may be shown in any performance events.

Movement

How the dog moves is the most extensively covered section of the standard. The German Shepherd Dog is a trotting dog. Gait is extremely important to the breed as a unique identifying factor and an integral part of his working ability.

The general impression is one of a working animal with an incorruptible character combined with body and

gait suitable for the arduous work that constitutes his primary purpose.

The AKC recognizes as a fault worthy of disqualification, regardless of the breed, any dog that attempts to bite the judge. Within the German Shepherd Dog breed they also disqualify any German Shepherd Dog with a docked tail, cropped or hanging ears, a nose that is not predominantly black, undershot jaw, monorchid (having only one testicle in the scrotum), or cryptorchid (retention of both testicles in the abdominal cavity), and any German Shepherd Dog that is white.

Under AKC rules a German Shepherd Dog will be excused for pronounced indications of deficiencies in character. (Examples include dogs that are too shy or aggressive to be examined by the judge.)

Serious faults as defined by the AKC standard also include tails that are too short or with clumpy ends due to ankylosis, any missing teeth other than first premolars, pale, washed-out colors, and blues—puppies born silver with gray overcoats as adults.

The AKC considers it a fault to have a soft, silky, or too-long outer coat, a woolly, curly, and open coat, or an unlevel topline with withers lower than the hips.

The Pedigree

If the standard is the light to the future, the pedigree is the gateway to the past. The integrity of the pedigree is in direct proportion to the integrity of the breeder and record keepers. This is an area where honesty and honor still play an important role. If the information on the pedigree is not honest and accurate, there is great potential for damage to the future of the breed.

The titles and degrees a dog obtains are of great significance to the breeder. They help establish the identity of the characteristics, skills, and abilities of a specific breed line. It would probably be impossible to attain all degrees and titles on one animal, but a mix of both in the first three generations helps guarantee the purity and integrity of the breed.

While the standard should be regarded as the light to the future, no enduring future can be built without knowledge of the past. Therefore, the pedigree becomes that gateway to the past. By listing all of the dog's ancestors, it gives the description of the gene pool from which that individual originated and suggests the possible outcomes of any given mating. It is not a perfect predictor, but it is certainly a much better indicator than simply guessing on the outcome when backgrounds are unknown. This is not an exercise in producing mix breeds, but in producing or duplicating an already established breed pattern.

There is often confusion of vocabulary when referring to titles, degrees, and awards. Title, as defined by the *New Webster Dictionary*, refers to prefixes that usually denote social dignity or status and would go before the person's name. In the dog world that would include Champion (Ch), Sieger (Sgr), and Grand Victor (GV). Degree, as defined by the *New Webster Dictionary*, indicates steps or stages in an ascending or descend-

ing series or process. Degrees are placed after the dog's name and would include all Schutzhund (Sch), obedience, tracking, herding, agility, working dog, and other earned performance degrees. All health and other information come after the degrees. See Appendix D for a list and description of degrees and titles.

Earned awards such as Register of Merit (ROM) go between degrees and health certifications and Award of Excellence are generally placed at the front of the dog's name.

A pedigree with only names gives potential breeders little information unless they are personally familiar with every dog on the pedigree for at least three generations. Even then, the information will be only superficial, since no certification of authenticity is evident. It is unreasonable to expect every dog on every pedigree to have all of the possible, or even desirable, degrees, titles, and health certificates (all together referred to as certifications) available. But a reasonable representation of those that are important to the survival of the breed's basic looks and characteristics is not only possible, but also extremely important.

AKC Pedigree Certification

On the American scene, there are numerous options. Since many of these have shortened forms, it often makes it difficult to interpret. Keeping in mind that the AKC is the largest and most widely recognized of the recording agencies, an AKC-certified pedigree is often the place to start researching a dog's past. However, only certifications gained through AKC-sponsored or -approved events will be listed. Also keep in mind that while certifications in the fourth and fifth generations are very nice, all of those genes can be diluted, if not completely lost, if they are not also present in the first three generations.

Additional research is often required to find out what other certifications the dog has that fall outside the AKC's domain unless the breeder has kept updated records.

Additional Titles and Awards

Following the dog's name can be a string of letters that grow increasingly confusing depending on the length and variety. Starting with the AKC titles, they are grouped into various types of performance events. Obedience, tracking, herding, working dog, and agility are the degrees that relate to the special abilities of the German Shepherd Dog and help establish if the characteristics are still present in the dog.

All of the national awards and health certifications are placed after the performance degrees.

The AKC lists OFA, CERF, and DNA on the official registration form, provided the dogs involved have been either tattooed or microchipped for positive identification. The newest thing is DNA testing, which is more conclusive proof of the dog actually being the offspring of the listed parents. Eventually, this will become a standard and should eliminate the current problem caused by unscrupulous people who sell dogs with papers that do not accurately reflect the dog's parentage. Most of these kinds of sales do not carry an extended pedigree as part of the original deal.

German certifications do not appear on AKC-certified pedigrees. They must be obtained from the breeder or researched through a pedigree service (several are listed in the classified section of *Dog World, German Shepherd Review*, and the Internet). There are a number of titles and conformation classifications, as well as many performance titles and breeding classifications.

In summary, the standard gives the guidelines for what the dog should look like and how he should act or behave. The pedigree tells you if his parents and past relatives did look that way and could, in fact, act that way. It does not guarantee that the progeny (all the puppies) will look or act that way, but it does increase the odds substantially in their favor.

Pedigree depth—the number of dogs on the pedigree certified for a particular characteristic—increases the likelihood of a recurrence of that characteristic in the offspring.

The breeding of purebred dogs is not an exact science. It is more like a game of dice, but the judicious breeder can, through careful loading, cause the dice to fall more often in the pattern he or she chooses.

Chapter Four

Choosing a German Shepherd Dog That Is Right for You

The Shopping List

One of the first things any prospective dog owner should do is make a shopping list. At the head of the list should be a brief summary of what you want the adult German Shepherd Dog to be in looks, temperament, ability, and place in your life. Without a good list, you may end up leaving out essential ingredients. You may see things as you go along that you want to add to your list. A list will make it easier to keep track of what you want your final package to contain and will help prevent impulse buying, which many times leads to trouble later.

Desired Physical and Mental Traits

Your first list should have an additional list of more specifically detailed components such as size, coat composition, color, and any markings you especially like or do not want. What is the extent of faults you will tolerate in temperament? What will happen if the dog turns out to be noise shy?

People shy? Or, conversely, overly aggressive? What if he doesn't like kids? (It happens.) Does this dog have to be play-oriented or would you settle for a good food-driven dog? Do you want both? Is this going to be a dog for all types of training? Or will you be happy if he follows you around and makes his major job in life keeping you company?

As you go along, leave room for additional comments. Nothing ensures future success as well as planning and setting goals. Many potentially good puppies grow up to be dogs that do not meet the owner's expectations. This is never the dog's fault. When selecting the puppy, the owner lacked a clear vision of what would be expected of the adult dog. All puppies are adorable; however, all puppies cannot grow up to be each individual's idea of the perfect dog. There is great variability in the final outcome of any puppy, but it is not infinite. Some selection must go into the initial consideration to help make the final outcome a reality.

Training and Socialization Time

The next section on your list should deal with the honest amount of time you have at your disposal to train and interact with the dog. No puppy can grow up to be your ideal dog without some personal input. Never get a dog with the intention of having someone else do your work. Only in specialized independence and support dogs does this type of situation work and only then because the handler later spends many hours learning how to work with the dog.

Time with the dog, even if only for basic obedience and socialization, will probably include some traveling.

Dogs trained only in their backyard are often the ones that make horrible mistakes in judgment on the rare times they are allowed out or happen to escape. Nearly all of the maulings and killings of small children were done by dogs with no formal training or outside socialization. Do not lie to yourself on this one. Make sure you have sufficient time and energy to plan and follow through with your program.

In addition to the time needed to socialize and train, even at the most minimal levels, there must be additional time for exercise and maintenance. Think carefully and define the level of activity you want in the adult.

This will help in your selection process.

The Crate

Most German Shepherd Dogs prefer to live in the house and this is the ideal situation. If you are able and can take your dog with you everywhere, that is perfect; however, most people cannot do this. So you need a safe, comfortable, secure place for your dog when you are away. A crate in the house until the dog is mature enough to be left alone for extended periods of time may be all you need. However, a nice outside run with shade and housing is most convenient. Portable kennels are easy to obtain and can be moved, camouflaged, or taken down for special events if your area is small.

The area the dog lives in at home should also be clean and free of parasites. All dogs need a comfortable, weather-protected place to sleep, with an ample area for exercise and elimination. No dog should ever be allowed to roam free. You might be leaving yourself open to legal action, not to mention exposing the dog to all manner of injuries and disease.

Chains

Along with not allowing your dog to run loose, confining him on a chain is an inexcusable and unacceptable policy. Chaining has been known to sometimes make even the most passive dog vicious and aggressive. And since chains do break, you are again putting yourself in a position that invites disaster and, possibly, legal action.

A Run

A safe run with some shade is advantageous for daytime airing, but a truly good dog is at his best when he lives in the house with the family. That was one point that Max Emil Friedrich von Stephanitz, the founder of the German Shepherd Dog breed and the Schutzhund movement in Germany, stressed in his book, The *German Shepherd Dog in Word and Picture*. Stephanitz emphasized the special need that German Shepherd Dogs have for human companionship in order to grow and develop to their fullest potential. While kenneling may be necessary in some circumstances, it should always be kept to the barest minimum possible.

Invisible Fences

Beware of the currently available "invisible fences." They may keep the dog from leaving, but there is no protection from outside dogs or people coming in and causing problems. The original intent of these buried fences was to keep dogs out of specific places (flower beds, ponds, driveways) inside a larger fenced area.

Spaying and Neutering

A spayed (sterilized by removing the reproductive organs) female is often calmer and easier to manage. The next best option is a neutered male (sterilized by removing the reproductive organs). Both spaying and neutering reduce the amount of upkeep considerably as well as extend the life of the dog by several years. A big killer of dogs, besides trauma, is cancer. Major cancers often occur in the reproductive organs.

Also figure into your time one or two trips yearly to the veterinarian for regular shots, worm checks, and a general checkup. Occasionally, other visits may be necessary for illnesses or emergencies.

Consider this a 15-year involvement/investment—look at the future carefully before you commit. If you do not have the time, energy, or ability to manage a high-powered competition German Shepherd Dog, face that fact before you select a puppy that might turn into a nightmare to live with as an untrained adult. For a companion dog, you want a stable, nonhyper, easy-to-train, loving dog.

Do not select a shy, retiring bundle of nerves to take home as a companion, as you will both probably grow farther apart with maturity instead of achieving the bond for which this breed is famous.

What Is Available

Next we will look at the extensive range of available German Shepherd Dogs both in this country and abroad. Exploring the vast range of characteristics in German Shepherd Dogs from different areas, kennels, and bloodlines is a challenging undertaking.

Because of the tremendous number of individuals within the German Shepherd breed, not only in America and Germany, but also around the world, there is going to be an enormous variability within the breed. There is also going to be a number of isolated pockets of breeding stock and gene pools that are relatively restricted to the area or location in which they are found.

Different groups have different needs and the different groups will emphasize the characteristics that fit those needs.

How to Find a Breeder/Seller

All too late many first-time German Shepherd Dog buyers have discovered that AKC registration is no guarantee of quality any more than having an automobile registered guarantee that it will give you dependable service for years to come. Dog buying in general is currently a "buyers beware" market in basically the same category as buying used cars. There are some sellers that are good and, then, there are some that are not.

There are a few general signposts that help determine which breeders/sellers are genuinely interested in the dogs and the future of the dog-and-owner team.

1. They ask informed and leading questions about where the dog will be housed and how much time will be spent with the dog.

2. They want to know the composition of the family, past history with pets, under what conditions you would dispose of the dog, and if you would be willing to keep in touch with the breeder.

All serious breeders have three-to five-generation pedigrees that go with each puppy as well as detailed feeding and maintenance schedules. These will include written records of all shots and medications up to the date

of purchase and dates when subsequent shots or medications are due.

Predictability

Breeders have generally graded the litter and have a good idea of which puppies are the most outgoing and which are more reserved. They make an honest effort to make the best match of each puppy with the future owners. They can also give you a fair prediction of what that puppy will be like as an adult based on past experience with similar litters. The predictability factor is one of the major reasons for pedigrees and planned breeding practices. In reality, the only true purpose of a controlled purebred breeding program lies in the predictability of the progeny.

Rescue and Shelter Options

Rescue dogs and humane shelter adoptees lack basic predictability. If you get a puppy, you have no idea what the adult dog will look like or how he will behave. With adults, there is a very high return factor on shelter adoptees in most cities. The problems that got them there in the first place often resurface after the novelty of the new home wears off in the first few days. If you are looking for a specific type of adult, these are very unlikely places to be successful.

The conformation and appearance of the dog should be taken into consideration when selecting an animal you intend to live with, train, and show to conformation titles or whatever degrees you choose.

Looks should not reflect a personal whim, but should be regarded as a factor in the dog's physical fitness for the work he was bred to do, plus an eye-appealing conformation to the specific standard of the breed. You will often hear people say they do not want a "show dog," just a companion or working dog. Yet they fail to realize that the conformation of the show dog is the outward manifestation of the dog's physical ability to do the job for which he was designed. The total dog will be the sum of his parts plus what the two of you bring to the relationship. If his parts are substandard, the final product will show the effect.

Suggestions and Warnings

Select a list of breeders by writing or going online to the German Shepherd Dog Club of America, the internationally recognized breed club that represents this breed, and ask for a list. Addresses of the national club can be found online and in the *American Kennel Club Gazette* available from the American Kennel Club (AKC), *Dog World* magazine, or other magazines that serve the dog fancy. Current addresses are in Appendix A of this book.

Never buy a dog from a kennel without visiting it or having recommendations from someone who has been there or knows the breeder through reputation. Most people would never buy a car over the phone or by writing, and a dog should last you many more years than most cars do. So consider this an investment that, while not necessarily a large initial capital expense, will certainly become one over the years in both time and money. Make it with as much care and deliberation as possible. Online Web sites can be beautiful covers over very unpleasant realities. Do your research and check references.

Price

One important consideration will involve the price limits of your budget. The average price range currently on a working pup with suitable body build and temperament to attain a UDT Sch III will be from $500 up to several thousand dollars, depending on the kennel, the location, and the background of the dog. Conformation prospects generally start around $800 but also can range well into the thousands depending on the kennel, the type of contract and guarantees, and the age of the dog at purchase. Good, sound companion dogs from reputable kennels generally start from $500 to $1,500 or higher, again depending upon the age and guarantees involved. Prices change over time, so check with your national club to determine the current value of good dogs. Paying a high price does not necessarily guarantee that you are getting either a good or suitable dog for you.

Do not bargain hunt for backyard breeder sales. It is too expensive in

both time and money to raise and train a dog to waste it all on an inadequate or substandard dog. No matter how lucky you are or how good a trainer you are, it is going to cost you several dollars before you get titles and/or degrees on your dog. Entry fees and travel expenses alone will be substantial, not to mention the food and medical bills and the training expenses as the dog matures. You won't spend any more on this than you would on any other hobby, but, be realistic. You wouldn't buy a "Saturday Night Special" to hunt elephants, so don't buy an adequate house pet and then expect him to hold up under the type of pressure necessary for competition.

Another excellent source of information can come from calling people who are currently involved with breeding and/or showing German Shepherd Dogs in the areas of your interest. Usually they will be most helpful and will give you the opportunity to meet several owners as well as their dogs. If all you are looking for is a companion, these are still excellent guidelines.

More Questions for Your List

1. Other things to consider include the ultimate size of the dog. Do you want a very large dog or one just big enough to do the job? Bigger is not always better, and beauty is always in the eye of the beholder. I prefer smaller females to work with. In my opinion, a spayed female is the ideal companion.

2. Do you want a dog that is easy to train, or one that presents a challenge? What are the specific legal aspects of owning a German Shepherd Dog in your area? In some areas there are no restrictions other than common sense and good judgment. In other areas, however, there are some very demanding laws and requirements. It is best to know in advance about the regulations and laws in the area in which you plan to live with this dog both today and in the future. This is a very mobile society. Be aware that the dog that is acceptable in your current area may be prohibited in some future relocation site. Far better to know this now than have to face unpleasant alternatives in the future. Most breeders can give you some worthwhile ideas and suggestions along these lines if you ask.

Going Shopping

When you have selected the breeder you want to visit, consider ahead of time what you are going to do and which questions you are going to ask. Some of these questions may even be used when you talk to the breeder to set up the appointment to see the litter. Screening such as this may save you unnecessary trips and valuable time.

A list of questions will help keep you on the right track and not let you be led astray by a cute puppy or a fast-talking breeder looking to make a quick sale. All puppies are cute, but only a few are born to be the adult dog of your specific dreams. First ask if the dog is AKC registered. The AKC regularly checks kennels for record compliance and responds to complaints against unethical practices. Sometimes these investigations lead to the withdrawal of all AKC privileges, including the right to register puppies with them. Since the AKC started doing DNA testing, many new registries have appeared on the scene. Most of these offer few if any benefits to their clients and none of them are recognized by the AKC, thus banning you from regular competitions in the thousands of events sponsored yearly by the AKC. Go online and check the advantages of the American Kennel Club. They support a wide variety of health research and help all dog owners in their current fight to maintain control of and ownership of their dogs.

Questions for the Breeder

1. You might be interested in knowing how the breeder came to select this combination of dogs (often referred to as a "line") for breeding.

2. Also, how many dogs from these bloodlines have been or are successfully working in the areas of interest to you?

3. What are the breeder's guarantees?

4. Will they be in writing?

5. If the breeder has none, would he consider a contract that you have drawn up?

6. Does the breeder belong to the national breed club? If not, why not? (Breed clubs have been known to

refuse membership to breeders who follow unethical breeding and business procedures.)

7. Does the breeder train or compete in the areas of interest to you?

8. What type of medical program does this breeder follow for both the adults and the puppies?

9. Have any dogs from these lines been sold to people who are competing successfully in any of the above competitions?

This may seem like a number of questions, but if you check these things out before you even look at the litter, you will often save yourself much time and many regrets in the future.

If all of the answers seem logical and accurate and lead you to feel that this breeder is interested in the dogs, in their future, and in what your goals are, then go look at the kennel and the puppies. Take stock of the overall appearance of the kennel. Is the whelping area clean and well ventilated? Do the mother and pups seem to radiate health and well-being? If available, look at the sire of the puppies. Many excellent breeders do not choose to maintain their own stud dogs, preferring to ship or take their bitches to the most suitable males for their purposes. However, the breeder should have good pictures of the stud dog and the genetic background information. You should also be able to learn the reasons for selecting that particular dog to mate with this particular bitch.

Note: Just because both the male and female are AKC registered does not necessarily make them a suitable mating pair.

Notice if the puppies are active and interested in what is going on around them. Is the mother protective without being vicious? Can the owner control her with voice commands, or does the bitch have to be restrained physically in order for you to see the puppies? If you are looking for a laid-back and highly social dog, an easy-to-control bitch would be desirable. On the other hand, a highly protective bitch might signal a strong drive and eagerness to protect.

Eight puppies make for a large litter for the average bitch to nurse, with four to six being more desirable. At six to eight weeks, obviously sub-standard puppies are readily identifiable. A puppy that is fearful or shy at this age is as crippled as one with a serious physical deformity.

Discuss with the breeder how a particular puppy does or does not meet the description of the standard. If a breeder cannot do this, in all probability this is not a show-quality litter. It is not a wise idea to buy a puppy for show potential without a second opinion from another reputable breeder or handler. If no one lives close enough to the litter to come and help you, make a video and send it for evaluation. This will be time well spent. Mistakes may still be made, but this procedure reduces both the number and severity of potential problems.

Testing Puppies for Their Potential

Once the puppy or puppies have been selected for conformation and/or performance, the next step is to test them for potential. Testing is not absolute, but it helps eliminate problems and often highlights both desirable as well as unwanted traits. It is one more tool in the selection process that many people have found extremely helpful.

Tests are more reliable if given during the sixth, seventh, or ninth week. If you plan to take the puppy home should he turn out to be the one you want, the seventh or the ninth week is best. The eighth week is a fear period for puppies, and things that happen during that time have a more pronounced effect on the puppy's later development than at other times.

Shy or retiring puppies rarely grow into stable adults. Temperamentally, your prospect should be a very alert, outgoing puppy, exhibiting some initial reserve with strangers, but no fear. Walk up to the litter, kneel down, and call the puppies. Watch how they approach you. Look for confidence, assurance, and boldness. Pick the most likely two or three. If one or more of these is of the sex you prefer, continue testing.

The first test should be to see if the puppy will take food from your hand. Use a small piece and hold it

You need to develop an understanding of how dogs learn and the philosophical foundation underlying Optimum Placement Technique (OPT). Whether you select your puppy and start from scratch or go with the dog you already have, every section of this book is important, but the chapter on puppy raising is essential.

in your palm with your hand open. Also see if the puppy can focus on the food if you drop it on the floor close to and in front of the puppy. You may have to show him the food the first time. The quicker the puppy picks up on these two actions, the easier he will probably be to train.

Look for an outgoing puppy that is not trying to dominate the rest of the litter. Above all, do not make the mistake of selecting the loner. Pick the two or three puppies that come to you most willingly, the ones that feel free to leave to explore something of interest but will return when you call them back.

You expect your dog to give you everything he is capable of giving. Do not short him by not doing your share. Training is a partnership, and, in a special and wonderful way, a unique sharing of time, adventures, and companionship. This book is designed to help you enjoy this wonderful experience to the fullest. Again, even if you are going no further than companion dog, all dogs need socialization, communication, and foundation training.

Chapter Five

Nutrition and Health

Feeding

Volumes have been written about feeding dogs, and there is still much controversy over which foods are best. The amazing number of new and experimental diets for dogs seems to expand at an alarming rate. The recall of several brands of food for problems has caused the public to experience uncertainty and confusion. At this point, the best sources for advice are probably the breeder you got your dog from and/or your veterinarian. As you feed your dog, keep a record of any problems you encounter. This will help you and your veterinarian come up with suitable diets that will address your dog's specific needs. Many dogs experience allergies to various ingredients in commercial foods; these concerns are best handled by your veterinarian. Keep records to avoid making the same mistakes repeatedly.

Dogs operate much like people in that a healthy diet, regular and appropriate exercise, and routine health checks lead to longer, more productive lives.

The Proper Diet

Many people argue that the dog is a carnivore and should be fed only meat. However, the dog is really an omnivore because when he devours his prey, he eats all parts of it—this includes the digestive system contents. In rabbits and small rodents, which make up the main menu of most wild canines, this usually consists of ingested vegetable matter.

A factor that is often overlooked is availability. Most people must select from those foods that are available within their area.

Remember, carbohydrates are cheap to produce and market. Proteins, and fats, are expensive to produce and formulate into feed. When you buy dog food, you generally get what you pay for. Cheap food is nearly always lacking in or inadequate in the essential life-building and -sustaining ingredients for the dog.

Foods lacking in nutrients the dog's body craves often cause the dog to overeat and become fat rather than healthy. Obviously, obesity is as bad for a dog as it is for a person. This condition stresses the same organs in dogs as it does in humans—heart, liver, kidneys, the musculoskeletal system, and the circulatory system.

A small amount of table scraps of stews, vegetables (except onions), and meats make healthy and enjoyable additions to a well-balanced diet. Avoid feeding your dog wild animals, regardless of how much he loves eating them. A high incidence of tapeworms, tularemia, and other diseases are present in the body and organs of many wild creatures.

Raw meat is a super food provided you observe strict sanitary control over its distribution. Most German Shepherd Dogs can process raw bones with little or no difficulty. However, never feed cooked bones to your dog, as their tendency to splinter will most likely cause internal punctures. The jury is out on the feeding of raw meat, especially bones, to dogs. Some feel it is worth the possible risks involved; others do not. The bottom line on dog food is no matter how much you study and research, you will probably never figure out whose food is the best on the market. But, you can figure out which food is best for your kennel or your dog.

An all-meat diet has several drawbacks. The most dangerous is the possible contraction of botulism or other harmful ingestible substances.

Keeping Food Clean

Prevention of communicable digestive diseases includes scrupulous cleanliness. Dishes should be

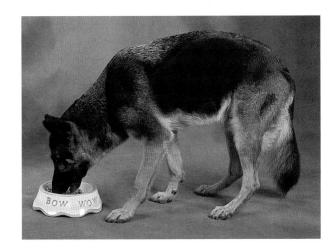

washed and scalded frequently. Fecal deposits must be removed from cages, runs, or lawns at least daily. Prepared foods should be kept refrigerated between feedings. Fresh food should be contained and handled with the same sanitation you would use for your family's food.

Feed your dog in a stainless steel or hard plastic bowl that will be easy to keep clean. Feed in a quiet place that is out of sight of other dogs. Even friendly dogs can be upset if they think there is a possibility of another dog getting their food. Environments that make the dog nervous during feeding could lead to an upset stomach. Some dogs prefer to eat in their crate where they feel safe and can relax.

Health Problems

One would like to think that a healthy German Shepherd Dog would be apparent on first glance,

Liquid medicine is easier to give with a syringe (no needle attached).

6. The insides of the ears should not show any inflammation (angry shades of red to pink), nor should there be any discharge or odor. Dirt, debris, or any type of internal secretions should not be present.

7. The teeth should be clean with no buildup of tartar.

8. There should be no unpleasant odor associated with the mouth.

9. Paws should be neat and clean with toenails almost back to the hairline. Check the pads for cuts or burns and the nails for breaks or damage.

Another area to check is the anal region. The area under the tail should be clean with no signs of inflammation, lumpy growths, or dried feces. Anal sac infections are extremely unpleasant for the dog. Dogs that scoot along on the rug or floor rarely have worms; this is the general reaction to problems in the anal area.

Infected or stopped-up sacs left untreated can lead to anal sac abscesses that rupture to the outside of the skin. Problems should be examined promptly by your veterinarian. Delay in repairing the damage can be both expensive for you and unpleasant for the dog.

but looks can be deceiving. Many dogs have serious problems that are not immediately visible.

In looking for a healthy German Shepherd Dog one should be able to observe an overall appearance of vitality and general well-being.

1. The coat should be resilient and clean, with no dry flaking, odor, or grease.

2. Healthy coats do not come out when pulled except during the seasons when the dog drops its undercoat.

3. There should be no sores, itchiness, or strong odors.

4. Also, there should be no sign of external parasites such as fleas, ticks, or lice.

5. The eyes should be clean and free of discharge with no redness or vision impairment.

Parasites

Parasites, both internal and external, are an ongoing problem with all dog fanciers. External parasites, including fleas and ticks, have become a greater problem in the past few years. The increasing mobility of our society, coupled with the neglect of dogs and letting them roam free, has carried these little monsters into places they were never seen before. Fleas cause itching, irritation, and extreme discomfort. And while they generally prefer dogs, they can make themselves right at home on humans. They can spread tapeworms, and cause anemia and flea allergy dermatitis.

Parasite Prevention

Prevention always must include treatment of the animal and environment, as well as maintaining a prevention program. There are products that you can apply directly to the dog and some that can be taken internally. It is always best to consult your veterinarian before applying or administering any form of parasite prevention. Chemical conflicts are always a potential threat.

Recent scientific studies have shown that neither B-vitamins, garlic, nor yeast has any repelling effect on fleas.

The effectiveness of feeding natural supplements such as herbs and other botanical products to keep fleas away has not been proven. Plus, some plants such as garlic can have adverse effects on some dogs. Long-term feeding of garlic has been shown to cause anemia in dogs by breaking down red blood cells.

Warning: Always consult your veterinarian before giving your dog any additional foods or supplements for any reason.

Tapeworms

With the flea has come its little passenger, the tapeworm. At one time, the tapeworm was relatively rare, but now it has reached near-epidemic proportions in many areas.

Most fecal examinations do not reveal tapeworm infestations, so they are difficult to diagnose. However, if you observe your dog's stools over a period of time, you may be lucky enough to catch sight of them. You may see white ribbon or threadlike flat segments or little white grains that look like rice in the stools. You may see this only once in a hundred stool samples of the same dog, but it always means the dog has tapeworms. Sometimes, when you check your dog's anal region you will see white ricelike grains. Only your veterinarian can give you drugs that are safe and effective against tapeworms.

Tapeworms can cause dull coats and make the dog eat as much as three times the food he would normally take. Generally, the dog will look like he needs a good meal after he has just eaten a big dinner. The description "unthrifty" comes to mind. If you pluck at the dog's outer coat and it comes easily away in your fingers, this is another possible indicator of tapeworms. However, that can also be a symptom of several other problems.

"Hot Spots"

Any of the parasites that cause itching may increase the possibility of the development of "hot spots." The sudden bald patch of skin that is wet, sore, and seemed to have grown overnight is a moist eczema or summer sore. Normal canine and human skin have millions of superficial, nonpathogenic (nondisease-producing) bacteria living quietly on their surface. For a hot spot to occur, something has to upset that normal balance allowing the usual nonpathogenic bacteria to reproduce, invade the skin, spread deep into the hair follicles, and give off toxins that cause further damage.

When things go wrong, the dog licks, bites, and tries to get relief. So while some of the damage is caused by the bacteria, some of it is also self-induced. The most common causes of hot spots include: moisture on the skin surface that doesn't get a chance to evaporate, beestings, tick, fly, or other insect bites, contact allergens, such as tree and weed pollens settling through the coat onto the skin, and scratches or abrasions.

Treatment consists of first getting the area dry. Using a hair dryer on and around affected spots is particularly helpful in drying up infected areas. Your veterinarian should recommend whether to apply a topical medication and, if so, what kind. Often antibiotics are given orally or by injection. Occasionally, corticosteroids are helpful to reduce swelling and itching. Anything that keeps the dog from chewing is helpful. Try to discover the cause and eliminate it.

Veterinarians routinely recommend clipping the area around the lesion. Shaving the coat can be a real problem if the dog is showing. Most veterinarians can present alternative treatments to avoid this problem if you let them know how important retaining the coat is to showing. Personally, I have treated many hot spots over the years and have never had to resort to shaving. Catching sores early is extremely important. If you are persistent, eliminate the source of the trouble, and use the prescribed treatment diligently, you will bring this problem under control.

Ticks

The tick is another parasite we are seeing more of, especially in the South. Any winter with no severe freeze is usually followed by a summer with an abundance of ticks. Dogs running loose pick them up in the woods and bring them into the living area, where they will multiply and take over. Both ticks and fleas can be transported into an otherwise clean environment by rabbits, stray dogs, and any wild or feral creature that happens to pass through your dog's running area.

Ticks are easy to see but rather difficult to remove, generally causing a sore that takes several days to heal. Dips are moderately successful. Special care should be taken to check your dog after each trip outside during the tick season. Several excellent once-a-month tick killers are now available. Ticks are especially dangerous as they carry diseases that can be fatal to both dogs and humans.

One of the great dangers is deer ticks, which can transmit Lyme disease to both dogs and people. Primarily causing arthritis, fever, and sometimes neurological symptoms, Lyme disease has the potential to be fatal if not caught and treated promptly. Dogs exhibit joint pain with lameness showing in one or more leg. The final results invariably involve joint and connective tissue damage and some neurological signs. People get circular red rashes, headaches, musculoskeletal pain, cardiac irregularities, and dizziness. Dogs cannot transmit Lyme disease, but they can bring the tick to you. There are several other tick-borne problems that can adversely affect the dogs. Some cause extreme soreness around the neck as well as other joints.

Heartworms

Heartworms are found in the heart and lungs of a dog and not in the intestines, as with other types of worms. Heartworms live inside the right ventricle of the heart. They can grow as long as 14 inches (35.5 cm) and often resemble thin spaghetti. The damage they cause is slow, cumulative, and can be fatal. They restrict blood flow and cause organ damage. Symptoms include coughing, labored breathing, and even heart failure.

Heartworms are transmitted by more than 70 species of mosquitoes. Virtually all dogs are at risk, even dogs that never go outside. It is through the bite of a mosquito that the tiny larvae, called microfilaria, are spread from dog to dog. When a mosquito bites a dog and deposits the larvae, they travel through the dog's tissues and eventually enter the heart and lungs. Successful prevention means keeping the dog on heartworm preventive medication every month.

All dogs should be tested negative for heartworms by your veterinarian before you start medication. A once-a-month dosage is the current recommended procedure. When you first start your dog on preventive medicine, if he has not been on it since puppyhood, you may notice a slight loss of efficiency in his ability to detect scents. Skip a few days and test him again. This is a temporary reaction and usually passes within a week. This loss of scenting ability is often seen after a variety of medications, but generally the scenting ability returns after the medication has "settled in" or is discontinued.

Roundworms

The most commonly recognized of the puppy parasites is the large roundworm. Adult worms may reach a length of 8 inches (20 cm), are white in color, and are easily seen when passed in the stools. Adult dogs can be infected but many adults have some immunity to roundworms. The biggest problem is these worms are often fatal in young puppies. Puppies are most often infested before birth through the migration of internal larvae in the maternal tissues.

Nursing puppies can pick up roundworm and hookworm larva from the mother's milk up to four weeks of age. Infested puppies often show a lack of growth and loss of condition. They have a dull coat and often are "potbellied." Worms may be vomited or voided in the feces. Infection may be followed by problems in the respiratory system. As with other parasites, secondary infection resulting from the lowered resistance caused by the worms is often the principal cause of death in puppies.

All fecal matter of both the lactating bitch and the puppies should be disposed of in a quick and sanitary manner. People can be infected only by ingesting the larvae that have hatched from eggs deposited in animal stool. Eggs can survive in the soil for months. If infected, larvae can migrate through a person's internal organs, producing a situation called visceral larval migrans. Most at risk would be young children engaged in such activities as eating dirt and playing in sandboxes.

Do not use any drugs on your puppies until you have consulted your veterinarian. Puppies may be wormed as early as two weeks; however, the average schedule is three times, starting at about three weeks, then worming every 14 days two more times, then worm again at 12 and 16 weeks. I generally worm the mother the first two times since she is cleaning up the puppies and has a high probability of infection.

Hookworms and Whipworms

Hook- and whipworms have become a major problem in the past few years. Dogs that roam are the chief culprits in the distribution of these dangerous internal parasites.

At least twice a year, every dog should have a stool sample examined by a veterinarian to determine if any parasites are present in the dog's system. If your dog is on a parasite control program, once-a-year examinations should be sufficient. Dogs applying for therapy dog certification are required to have a yearly parasite check.

Hookworms attach themselves to the dog's intestinal lining, leaving bleeding internal wounds. They cause blood loss, anemia, and diarrhea. As few as 100 hookworms can kill a puppy.

Eggs pass through the feces of an infected dog. Once the eggs hatch into larvae, they can be picked up as part of the day's accumulated dirt. If the dog licks himself to clean up, these larvae may be swallowed. In some instances, the larvae may even penetrate through a dog's feet. This is an excellent reason to not let a dog wander about, especially where stray or roaming dogs could have contaminated the area.

Whipworms, shaped like whips, live in the large intestine. These parasites cause bloody diarrhea, anemia, dehydration, and loss of appetite. A female whipworm can produce 2,000 eggs a day. Eggs are passed in feces and can survive for years in the soil. They are very difficult to eradicate.

Coccidiosis

Rarely mentioned because at one time it was associated with conditions of poor sanitation and overcrowding, coccidiosis is becoming much more common throughout the country. This protozoa invades and destroys the intestinal mucosa and is frequently the culprit in young puppies that have diarrhea, loss of vitality, and poor resistance to other diseases. Coccidia are sometimes difficult to find, as they may not be present in every stool sample. Sometimes two or three checks are needed to identify it.

Coccidiosis can also become apparent after the stresses of weaning, shipping, sudden changes of feed, or severe weather. Coccidia are especially dangerous in young puppies. The lowered resistance opens the puppy to many life-threatening problems such as parvo, distemper, and pneumonia. Adults generally have no problems with these protozoa; however, they stand as the sources of infection to younger, more susceptible puppies.

The one characteristic of this annoying problem is that there is virtually no way to completely clean an environment once the coccidia protozoa has taken up residence. The general rule seems to be if you have ever had one case on your property, check every puppy from that time on for coccidia. Around four to six weeks is the safest time to make that first check. If the puppy does not have any, check again in a week or at any time signs of diarrhea appear until the puppy is three or four months old.

The basic treatment is Albon in liquid or tablet form, given according to puppy weight, for 10 days. Occasionally the treatment has to be repeated before the puppies are completely clean. Keeping the environment clean and dry, disinfecting everything including the feeding and watering stations, slows reinfestation and helps prevent other problems from developing. Since fecal material is a major carrier and puppies tend to put everything they come into contact with into their mouths, frequent cleaning is of primary importance. Working closely with your veterinarian is essential to both locate and treat this problem.

Do not attempt to treat dogs that have projectile, bloody, or painful vomiting, or explosive diarrhea. These are symptoms of serious internal problems. Blood coming from any orifice is an immediate danger sign. Most other symptoms of developing problems are slower in evolving and give you some time to address the situation.

Inoculations

Compared to the number of infections available to people, those transmitted from dog to people are relatively few and infrequent; those transmitted from people to the dog even rarer. The easiest to get are probably the easiest to prevent. Most infectious diseases found in both humans and dogs can be prevented by vaccination, good hygiene, proper food preparation, regular worming, and wearing protective clothing when necessary.

All dogs should be given a yearly inoculation for rabies and the combi-

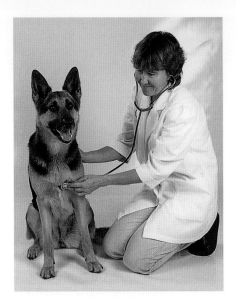

cats, foxes, skunks, and raccoons. Rabies is generally transmitted through some form of bite; however, there are cases where viral contamination is gained through fresh, already-existing wounds. A virus may be present in the saliva and be transmitted by an infected animal several days prior to the onset of clinical signs. Incubation is generally within 15 to 50 days; however, it may last even up to several months.

Rabid animals exhibit typical signs that are divided into three phases: the prodromal (the first one to three days), the excitative (often called furious or mad-dog rabies), and the paralytic. (The excitative stage is short or absent and the animal quickly becomes paralyzed.) In any animal, the first sign is a change in behavior, which will be different from such problems as digestive disorder, injury, poisoning, or an early infectious disease. Animals usually stop eating and drinking and may seek solitude. After the prodromal stage, animals quickly move to paralysis or become vicious. Sometimes the animal becomes irrational and viciously aggressive, pupils dilate, and noise invites attack. Dogs rarely live beyond 10 days of onset. Puppies often appear very playful, but bite more than usual, becoming vicious within hours.

Rabies can best be controlled through countrywide vaccination (this is the single most effective measure), and the elimination of stray dogs and cats that can become potential carriers. The most common carriers of

nation shot for distemper, Adenovirus Type 2 (covers hepatitis), and the parainfluenza and parvovirus complexes (DAPP). It is not advisable to give leptospirosis shots to young puppies unless it is epidemic in your area.

The best advice concerning health care protocol for your German Shepherd Dog lies with your veterinarian. The two of you should consult from the beginning on what your puppy or dog needs to maintain a regular and ongoing program of prevention and maintenance. The schedules of checkups and inoculations that should be given change as new research becomes available and can be introduced to the public at large.

Rabies

All warm-blooded animals, including people, are susceptible to rabies. It is carried mainly by bats, dogs, rabies are wild animals, the skunk being by far number one. Raccoons, foxes, and bats are also frequent carriers.

Annual rabies shots are the law in most states. A few states require shots only every two or three years with a vaccine that has been proven effective for three years and approved for such use. Unvaccinated dogs bitten by a known rabid animal should be euthanized immediately and the head sent for rapid laboratory evaluation. Because of the fatal nature of rabies, it is a much better idea to keep all rabies shots up to date starting with the four- or five-month-old puppy and continuing annually. It is strongly recommended that all veterinary practitioners and others exposed to random animal populations receive preexposure immunization.

Distemper

Distemper is a highly contagious, worldwide viral disease characterized by varying elevations of temperature, extreme gastrointestinal and respiratory distress, frequently leading to pneumonia, and neurological complications. Severe dehydration often results rapidly from excessive and often explosive diarrhea. Since the virus is airborne and infected dogs may shed the virus for several months, isolation and sanitation is of extreme importance in the prevention of further contamination. Although dogs may recover from distemper, there are sometimes long-term health problems involving a wide range of body functions.

Most often associated with puppies, distemper can attack any dog of any age if his immunity is low. Supportive care with IV fluids, vitamins, dextrose, and antibiotics might help to strengthen the dog in the hope that the dog will be able to produce his own antibodies to the virus. If the dog survives, he will have lifetime immunity. Modified live vaccines are the only option as research has shown that killed or inactivated vaccines for distemper do not provoke the animal to produce proper immune levels.

The best treatment is prevention. Shots should be given starting at six to nine weeks of age and continued every two or three weeks until after the fourth month. Keep the puppy free of all parasites and maintain a sanitary, warm, and dry environment. Feed the puppy a good-quality puppy food at least three times daily.

Parvovirus

Primarily a puppy problem, parvovirus is enteritis of acute onset with varying morbidity and mortality that can attack dogs of any age. Major transmission is through the ingestion of fecal material from infected animals. Puppies eating each other's feces or anything that has been exposed to infected fecal matter such as grass, sticks, leaves, or toys is the major route of infection. However, licking feet after walking through contaminated areas is equally effective in spreading parvovirus. One of the major problems is that the virus remains viable for years outside the host. It can be brought to the dog initially by human hands, clothing, milk, food, or any contaminated object. Parvovirus, because of its ability to live in the environment for long periods, is often spread by unsuspecting owners or visitors. Even stray dogs that venture into the dog's area could be carriers.

Any vomiting, hemorrhagic diarrhea, rise in temperature, or combination of these symptoms should be cause for alarm. Rapid diagnosis and treatment is often successful. If the puppies are not treated, death may follow as a result of dehydration, electrolyte imbalance, endotoxic shock, or secondary infections.

Puppies free of worms and coccidia seem to be less prone to infections of all types. Today's shots are extremely effective in prevention provided they are given on schedule. The vast majority of cases seem to be in puppies that were never vaccinated or are past due for boosters.

Canine Infectious Tracheobronchitis (CITB)

Canine Infectious Tracheobronchitis (CITB) is a contagious respiratory disease of dogs characterized by severe bouts of coughing. The cough may last from several days to weeks and generally spreads through the canine population rapidly. Although frequently called "kennel cough," CITB actually refers to any of a variety of respiratory infections that cause coughing. All dogs, especially puppies, should be treated with a vaccine. Most combination shots cover Adenovirus Type 2 and parainfluenza. Parainfluenza vaccines offer one guard against canine pneumonia.

Bordetella inoculation can be given as a shot or an intranasal vaccine. The intranasal is squirted up into one side of the animal's nose and offers quicker protection than the shot. Both adults and puppies as young as two to three weeks can receive initial inoculation. In areas of low incidence, 8 to 12 weeks would be sufficient. Yearly boosters are recommended. This, along with routine disinfecting and good ventilation, will help to control CITB (kennel cough) in your litters and adult dogs. New dogs entering the kennel should have been immunized at least two weeks prior to arrival.

While generally not life-threatening, if contracted, the cough, which is accompanied by a nasal discharge, can lead to fatal bronchopneumonia in puppies and debilitated adult or aged dogs. It tends to spread rapidly among animals that are closely confined. Stress and environmental factors such as cold, drafts, and high humidity apparently increase susceptibility. Many times the history includes stress or the exposure to an unfamiliar dog population such as a recent visit to an animal hospital, boarding or grooming kennel, or a show. If CITB has spread through a kennel, the premises may have to be evacuated for two weeks and disinfected. This is a much easier problem to prevent than to deal with after it gets entrenched.

Infectious Canine Hepatitis (ICH)

Infectious canine hepatitis (ICH), a contagious disease of dogs, has signs varying from a slight fever and congestion of the mucous membranes to severe depression, lowered white blood count, and prolonged bleeding. The current vaccination Adenovirus Type 2 combines protection from hepatitis and other CITBs. It is an improvement over the old hepatitis vaccines that often caused opacities of the cornea (one or both eyes) and were shed in the urine. Most puppies become immune to ICH when vaccinated at 9 to 12 weeks of age. Adults should receive boosters yearly or as the veterinarian recommends.

Leptospirosis

In addition, some form of yearly inoculation should be given for leptospirosis if the dog is going to be traveling into or is exposed to areas of possible infestation. The lepto element of the DHLPP shots given traditionally to puppies and to adults as boosters is no longer being given by many veterinarians. Dogs that travel frequently, especially to dog shows, should however, receive yearly lepto inoculations. Because many veterinarians are now using multiple yearly boosters that do not contain the lepto vaccines, it is increasingly up to the individual owner to request this booster be given.

Puppies receive a certain titer (immunity to all diseases that are vaccinated against) from their mother at birth. During the first 16 weeks of their life this immunity disappears. Only expensive titer tests can tell you when this happens. Shots are not effective so long as the puppy still holds natural immunity. Since you don't know when the titer falls to zero, there is a shot schedule (generally worked out between you and the veterinarian) that will maximize the probability that one of them will hit the puppy and grant immunity. The major fact to remember is that clinically, all natural immunity should be gone from the puppy's system sometime after 16 weeks. The shots given to dogs after four months are considered valid. Thereafter, a booster every year or two (depending upon the recommendation of your veterinarian) should be sufficient.

The practice of holistic medicine is gaining an increasingly wider acceptance among the medical profession, and many veterinarians are questioning the need for the number and frequency of previously recommended shot schedules. Consult your veterinarian for the latest updates as they occur.

Infections and Diseases

Brucellosis

Unaltered (not spayed or neutered) animals brought into frequent contact with a variety of other dogs should also receive yearly tests for brucellosis (both male and female). Also, females should be checked for vaginal infections on a regular basis. Current research indicates that there is a decided rise in the occurrence of brucellosis, a venereal disease transmitted by a coccabacillus bacterium that both dogs and people can contract. At present there is no known cure. Spaying or neutering a young dog seems to be the current suggested method of control of this problem. Also, keep them from roaming where other dogs may have eliminated, as brucellosis can be spread through the dog making contact with infected feces. Infection may also be transmitted through contact with semen, blood, tissue, milk, or urine from recently infected dogs, and possibly from other bodily secretions. If you are handling any material, fetal or placental, following an abortion in one of your bitches, wear gloves.

The primary symptom of brucellosis in dogs is abortion or infertility, but in humans it also includes constant weakness, fatigue, fever, chills, sweating, insomnia, sexual impotence, constipation, headache, joint pain, "nerves," and poor appetite. Because this is one of the several bacteria that is transmitted from dog to man, it is important to keep the dog away from possible sources of contamination. Spaying and neutering help prevent the transmission. There are no vaccines available and no known cure. Infected animals must be euthanized or permanently isolated.

Gingivitis

Gingivitis is probably one of the most common mouth problems in dogs. This acute and often chronic inflammation of the gums is characterized by congestion and swelling. If left untreated, gingivitis evolves into periodontitis, which destroys the support of the tooth within the jaw. This condition is seen with increasing frequency as the dog ages and is the result of lack of early and ongoing dental care.

German Shepherd Dogs should have a scissors bite, where the upper incisors overlap a bit and touch the lower incisors. An uneven bite may cause undue wear on teeth crowns. Jaws that are out of line causing the teeth to overlap on the sides of the mouth can lead to severe dental problems. Missing or misplaced teeth may or may not be problematic beyond the aesthetics and conformation showing limitations.

So long as the dog has a normal scissors bite and most of his teeth, he will survive well as a pet. However, the further away from normal an animal gets, the higher the probability of health problems. Therefore, all breeding stock should have healthy teeth in every respect.

Other Potential Problems

There are many other problems plaguing today's canine population: They suffer from heart disease and cancer, as well as liver, spleen, blood, eye, skin, feet, and bone problems that were not often recognized and identified in the past.

Keep your veterinarian informed if your dog develops any type of fits, convulsions, or seizures. A staggering gait, partial or complete paralysis, behavioral changes, or loss of balance may signal other nervous disorders. There are numerous medicines available for controlling these problems.

Warning signs for possible skin disorders include persistent scratch-

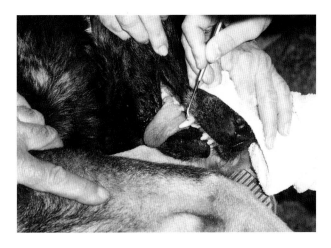

ing, increased hair loss, redness, or inflammation. These occurrences may be symptomatic of several problems, among them sarcoptic mange that is highly contagious, and demodectic mange that is much less so. Mange is a skin disease caused by parasitic mites.

There is a major difference between demodectic mange and sarcoptic mange. Demodectic mange though not contagious from dog to dog, or dog to human, is passed down from the mother to the puppies while nursing. It is advisable to spay or neuter any puppies that are positive for demodectic mange, as well as their mother. Juvenile demodectic mange may clear up, and stay in remission permanently, after treatment with topical and oral medications prescribed by your veterinarian. Recurring demodectic mange must be aggressively managed and may reach a point where treatment offers no relief and euthanasia is the only remaining alternative. Sarcoptic mange is intensely pruritic (itchy) and extremely contagious to people. Found worldwide, sarcoptic mange is transmitted by direct contact with infected animals—one more excellent reason to not let your dog wander about unsupervised. Stray dogs carry a great deal of unwanted baggage that they are more than happy to share with yours.

Bladder problems could be signaled by blood in the urine, straining to pass urine, incontinence, increased urination, and/or increased thirst—still another good reason to not let your dog wander. You need to be aware of his daily elimination habits in order to spot problems before they become life threatening. Many dogs kept outside are often seriously ill before the owner catches the symptoms. Dogs living in the house are generally observed in the earlier stages of a problem where treatment is both easier and more likely to be successful.

Bone, Muscle, and Joint Disorders

Bone, muscle, and joint disorders are often suspected when the dog becomes lame or starts to limp. Swelling around joints, tenderness when legs or hips are touched, and even paralysis are all warning signs. While hip dysplasia (HD) is by far the most commonly recognized of the bone disorders, it is by no means the only one. A number of front leg disorders, including elbow dysplasia

and nongenetic injuries, will all produce similar symptoms. Not all hip or rear problems are HD—there are several types of lameness that can be caused by injury. Luxating patella, while rare in German Shepherd Dogs, can also cause difficulty in sitting and negative reactions when the rear is pushed down. The inability of the knee joint to bend at times when the patella is out of line can be very painful.

There seems to be a connecting thread between orthopedic problems. To date, there has been no specific gene mapped as being the marker. Hip dysplasia is one manifestation of a genetic weakness resulting in one or more forms of osteochondrosis. "Osteo-" refers to bone, and "chondro-" to cartilage, especially in joints. So, osteochondritis is an inflammation in a joint. Very often, a dog with hip dysplasia will be found to have joint disease in different locations as well.

OCD

Osteochondritis dissecans (OCD) of the lower end of the upper arm, and similar conditions in the stifle and hock joints occur more often in some breeds than in others. Elbow dysplasias include ununited anconeal process, which is most often associated with German Shepherd Dogs. Getting elbows OFA certified (see Appendix D) should help reduce the occurrence of these problems within your breeding program.

Controlling weight gain and exercise during the early development is extremely beneficial as this is the period during which the acetabulum (the cup into which the leg bone fits) is solidifying. Placing excess stress upon this joint prior to total calcification can cause the formation of a shallow acetabulum, thereby increasing the chance for eventual hip displacement.

There has been a gradual change in the overall structure of the German Shepherd Dog since its earliest conceptions. There has been a gradual weight increase in both dogs and bitches. Also, there has been an increase in chest depth and a decrease in forelimb length. While not documented, it is speculated that these changes may have some bearing on increased frequency of orthopedic disease in the modern German Shepherd Dog. It is equally likely that breeding for looks and quick sales may have had even more impact as those types of breeders rarely screen for any genetic problems including those of an orthopedic nature. Any form of genetic problem can be reduced or controlled only through a careful screening of all breeding animals. Uncontrolled mating reproduces all of the available bad genetic problems both randomly and with increasing frequency. The only purpose of a breeding program should be ability to predict what the puppies will become when they grow up. And the prediction should be for soundness of mind and body as a first priority. All other characteristics should then follow the standard or blueprint for that particular breed.

Feed a well-balanced puppy food to assure adequate nutrition and a slow growth rate and limit the puppy to short periods of exercise. This is especially important during the first six to eight months of life. Do not give megadoses of anything, especially calcium, as this tends to make many more problems than it cures. The key to success in vitamins and minerals is the correct amount and the appropriate balance.

Lameness

Young dogs often experience "growing pains," which is, in fact, a form of eosinophilic panosteitis (eopan or pano). Pano causes lameness of German Shepherd Dogs between 5 and 16 months of age. There is no known cause. While bacteria, virus, fungus, or even heredity have been suggested as causes, none of these has been proven conclusively.

Pano may have a sudden or gradual onset of signs. Limping may be very mild and hardly noticeable, or it may be severe to the point of carrying the leg off the ground. Sometimes the lameness can shift from one leg to another in a short period of time. Lameness may persist for as little as a week or two or may occur over a year-long period. Only rarely does a dog show signs past 18 months of age.

Once other causes of lameness are ruled out, it becomes a matter of damage control, as there is no real cure other than time. If the lameness is mild and of short duration, no treatment is required. However, if

It is rarely a good idea to give dogs medicine designed for humans. Always check with your veterinarian before giving any medicines to your dog and be advised of new and developing techniques for the prevention and control of these problems.

lameness is more severe or lasts longer than two weeks, some form of medication should be used to make the dog feel better and help prevent otherwise nonused muscles from atrophying (shrinking).

Newer pain medicines have recently become available that are formulated specifically for dogs. Before these, dogs were given drugs developed for humans.

When German Shepherd Dogs Get Old

German Shepherd Dogs start to get old around 10 or 11 years of age. Often they begin to lose interest in sports and games that require a great deal of energy. They frequently develop a greater intolerance of heat, cold, or change in their lives.

Sometimes they start losing control of their bladder and bowels. Often they are more prone to illnesses. Moderate exercise, a comfortable resting place with adequate shade and shelter, a diet designed for seniors, and lots of love will let

your dog live out his golden years in quiet contentment.

Degenerative Myelopathy

Degenerative myelopathy (DM), a neurologic disease found mostly in German Shepherd Dogs, causes progressive spinal ataxia (muscular incoordination) and weakness. The most striking symptom is the reduction of rear limb and caudal axial musculature. While exercise is important to maintain muscle tone and circulation, vitamins E and B may delay DM symptoms. As with most problems, early detection and treatment give a greater chance of positive response. Minimizing stress is of basic importance. Surgery is not recommended because the degeneration caused by surgical stress may be irreversible.

German Shepherd Dogs are, on the whole, a rather healthy breed. However, individually, they can have any specific problem depending upon the breeding, nutrition, and environment of that particular dog.

There are many types of problems that can lead to illness that are not visually detectable. Some do produce discernible symptoms, but others may linger some time before becoming obvious unless you are watchful of your dog's behavior.

Cancer

A survey conducted by the Morris Animal Foundation indicates that cancer is very near the top of disease-related killers in dogs. Cancer

in dogs is as scary and unpredictable as it is in people. However,
research does indicate there are a
few precautions that can be taken.

1. Since dogs can absorb substances through their pads, it would
be wise to keep them out of yards
and fields that have been treated
with any type of chemical as well as
any potentially polluted water.

2. Some carpets are treated with
chemicals that have the potential to
be carcinogenic (capable of causing
or triggering cancer), so a plastic
kennel or separate dog bed is advisable.

3. Things they eat also can have
some cancer relationship, so a safe
diet would include a good grade of
dog food with as few dyes and
preservatives as possible and as little "junk food" as practical.

Dogs have all of the same types of
cancer as people; however, with their
inbred high pain thresholds, it is
sometimes easy to miss the early
signs. Spaying and neutering helps
eliminate cancers common to the
reproductive organs. Stay alert for any
lumps, sores, or unusual discharges.

Treatment consists of surgery,
radiation, chemotherapy, and hor-
mone therapy. Unfortunately, very little extends the dog's life more than a
year or two.

Advances in cancer research may
one day lead to better detection and
treatment for both dogs and people.
Until then, your veterinarian is your
best source for both diagnosis and
treatment.

German Shepherd Dogs are a relatively healthy breed, but the key to
long-term survival currently lies in

Pilling a Dog

There are three ways to give pills to a dog. The easiest is to conceal the pill in a bit of food.

1. First give the dog a decoy (piece of food, no pill), and then give the piece with the pill. Follow that quickly with another bite to make sure your dog swallows the piece with the pill.

2. The second way is to open the dog's mouth and drop the pill all the way to the back, then close the mouth, keep holding the head up, and stroke the throat until the dog swallows.

3. The last resort is to open the mouth and place the pill all the way back and partly down the dog's throat. Again, hold the dog's head up, mouth closed, until he swallows.

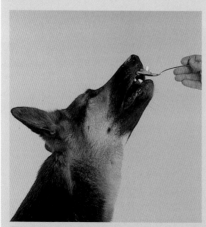

The easiest way to give a dog medicine is to conceal it in a bit of food.

awareness and prevention on the part of the owner.

Bloat

Mention bloat in a group of German Shepherd Dog owners and the stories start to roll. You would think every other German Shepherd Dog is a target, but statistically this is not true. Many breeds suffer equal, if not higher, rates of occurrence.

Bloat or gastric torsion, also called gastric dilation-volvulus (GDV), is a complex disorder that generally occurs as a life-threatening emergency. Speed of diagnosis and treatment is often the key factor in saving the dog's life. GDV is characterized by expansion of the stomach with gas or frothy material. Rotation (volvulus) may or may not occur. If it does, the entry and exit from the stomach are effectively closed. The most obvious symptom is an unusually distended abdomen. The dog often attempts to vomit without producing anything, along with excess salivation. Speed in starting treatment is the key factor. When these symptoms are present, call your veterinarian immediately.

One of the tragedies of kennel dogs or dogs that are housed somewhere outside is they often bloat during the night when there is no one around to see and react and are generally dead by the next morning. Dogs that sleep close to their owners have a better chance of waking them as they become restless and uncomfortable in the early stages of bloat.

A great deal of research has been done in the field of canine bloat, and while excessive exercise around mealtime, overeating, and overdrinking should be avoided, the actual cause of bloat in specific animals is still undetermined.

Some breed lines seem to have a greater incident than others do. Hereditary influences, which relate to physiologic control of the stomach, may exist and should be considered when selecting dogs for breeding. Dogs with a history of GDV in their backgrounds might benefit from being fed two or three small meals daily rather than one large meal. Actually, if possible, three daily feedings represents a more desirable feeding schedule for the German Shepherd Dog.

Pancreatitis

Pancreatitis is often brought on by the sudden eating of a high-fat meal or gorging on any type of foods; this is especially dangerous in obese and/or sedentary dogs. Chicken and turkey skins given as treats around Thanksgiving and Christmas are frequently followed by attacks of pancreatitis. Symptoms include depression and sudden vomiting of undigested food several hours after eating, followed by thirst and increased water intake. Diarrhea is common and, combined with the vomiting, can lead rapidly to dehydration.

Prompt diagnosis and treatment generally leads to long-term recovery, especially in mild cases. Where there is acute destruction of the pancreas, and especially if there is hemorrhage, the outlook is much poorer and the fatality rate can be moderate to high. The cases in between that are less clear-cut are those most likely to cause recurrent problems. These often lead to repeat attacks of acute pancreatitis, occasional cases of diabetes, and the possibility of permanent, chronic pancreatitis.

Heatstroke

Heatstroke is often the result of dogs being left in an overheated environment (car, furnace room, hot sun, unventilated crates in hot areas) or overworked on extremely warm days. Another typical scenario for heatstroke is a dog tied or chained that gets tangled up in hot weather and struggles to get free until he succumbs to heatstroke. Typical signs of heatstroke are weakness, collapse, rapid heartbeat, and gums that are pale or bright red. Your dog's temperature should be checked and if it is elevated, you should use the water treatment suggested below to bring it down.

Water Treatment

When taking the temperature, be sure to put sufficient lubricant, as the rectal area is often very dry. Any temperature over 106°F (41°C) should be considered dangerous. The best treatment is to immediately get the dog into cool or tepid water. A bath-

Taking a Dog's Temperature

There are times when you may need to take the dog's temperature. Never attempt to take the temperature in the mouth. Using a rectal thermometer (baby or human), insert it into the rectum about two or three inches. Putting K-Y Jelly or Vaseline on the thermometer helps reduce the discomfort of inserting it. Leave the thermometer in for about a minute, comforting and steadying the dog during this process. It is painless but the dog may need to be slightly restrained. If the dog becomes agitated, wait until you are at the clinic and let the veterinarian do it. In most cases, if the dog is sick enough for you to need to take his temperature, he will let you. The normal temperature range of a dog is between 100.5°F and 102.5°F (38–39°C).

ing around and through them and that they are in the shade. Never leave the dog outside where there is no shelter available. Keep adequate water on hand, especially during hot weather.

German Shepherd Dogs enjoy air conditioning just as much as we do. However, moving the dog from a cold interior out into the heat, especially when he is expected to work, can be very stressful on his respiratory system. A cool spot to set the crate, even with a fan set to circulate air around the dog, makes it easier for him to maintain his temperature balance.

Burns

Electric burns, especially from puppies and dogs chewing through electric cords, are more common than realized by most people. Sometimes the animal receives a minor burn and simply doesn't repeat the transgression. However, the burn can be very severe, even causing death. Burns can be cleaned with cold water, after which you should rub in a bland first aid cream. The problem with electricity is the damage may be greater than it appears at first. One common problem following electrical cord shock is difficulty in breathing due to fluid buildup in the lungs. Internal damage may be sufficiently severe, resulting in death three or four days later. The basic rule to follow is if your dog receives a shock, take him to your veterinarian immediately.

tub, child's swimming pool, or water hose can be used. The rectal temperature should be monitored every five minutes until it drops below 104°F (40°C). At that point it is safe to stop the water treatment. However, in most cases it is best to call the veterinarian and seek additional advice.

Prevention

As with most emergencies, the best treatment is prevention. Do not leave any dog in a car unsupervised, especially in the summer. Make sure all crates have plenty of air circulat-

For any severe burn, either from fire or chemicals, get the dog to the veterinarian as quickly as possible. Do not douse your dog with water as you would with a minor burn and do not try to treat the burned area. Dehydration and shock are major dangers in severe burns. Professional care should be sought immediately.

Bites

Animal bites vary from superficial to severe. If possible, clean the wound and leave it open. Apply a first aid cream on or in small puncture wounds. If the wound is large or in a place that might be difficult to heal, sutures may be necessary. All deep wounds—and any wound at all over the abdominal area—should be seen by a veterinarian. Even a small puncture wound over the abdomen could possibly have punctured the intestinal tract and be life threatening in a short period of time.

All cat bites should be seen by a veterinarian, as there is no bite more likely to become infected than a cat's bite.

Removing Foreign Objects

Dogs will eat an astounding variety of things. They often become the victims of their own curiosity, greed, carelessness, and, in some cases, even cruelty. A dog the size of a German Shepherd Dog can swallow

something as large as a tennis ball, and smaller balls are much easier. These nearly always require surgery to remove.

Dogs living near water have many problems related to fishhooks. Careless fishermen who leave bait, particularly casting plugs, on their lines and then leave their poles where dogs can get at them present an especially dangerous lure. Sometimes the barbs get hooked in the lips, nose, eyelids, and even the tongue of the animal. If

If your dog gets into any woods, the possibility of encounters with interesting creatures such as porcupines exists. Porcupine quills in the nose or mouth are very painful and most animals must be anesthetized in order to remove the quills. The dog should probably then be placed on a long-lasting antibiotic to be on the safe side against infection.

Metal tags, safety pins, barbed wire, needles and pins, pieces of plastic wrap, and sausage casing can often lead to serious problems once in the stomach. Most dogs will vomit, refuse food, have scanty or bloody stools, and be unable to retain water if foreign objects are ingested.

Bones or pieces of wood can become lodged crosswise in the roof of the mouth. Many can be removed by the owner, but if it has become firmly lodged it is safer to have the veterinarian remove it.

The basic rule of thumb is, if your dog is acting strangely, have him examined by a competent veterinarian. Do not wait, since the situation generally only gets worse and the animal will suffer for a longer period of time than necessary.

Poisons

Most people do not realize the extreme availability to dogs, especially puppies, of things that can poison them. Just to list a few:
- alcohol
- beer (it is not cute to try to get your dog drunk; it can lead to staggering and coma)

the dog panics, even more damage may be done. Cut the dog loose and get him to the veterinarian as quickly as possible.

If your dog is loose at any time unsupervised, even in your yard, BBs and/or birdshot can become a problem. Sometimes it is the result of cruelty, but it is more often someone in frustration trying to keep a dog away from their property or stock. When you stroke your dog, you may find these types of pellets under the skin. They can easily be removed by the veterinarian.

- antifreeze and deicers (they are sweet and dogs love them)
- any aspirin-related drug (can cause depression, weakness, and/or vomiting)
- bleach
- chocolate
- caffeine (small amounts in a dog as large as a German Shepherd Dog are generally not too serious but can cause hyperacidity and vomiting)
- detergent and ammonia, dish laundry detergents, and shampoos
- drain cleaners
- fertilizers
- any fuels
- volatile cleaners and solvents
- insecticide
- perfumes
- marijuana
- strychnine
- snow/ice salts
- weed killers (which they can absorb through their pads, especially just after a rain shower).

Chocolate is at least mildly poisonous to dogs and should never be used as a treat. As little as 4.3 ounces of unsweetened chocolate would be a fatal amount for a 40-pound (18 kg) dog. Even small amounts may cause vomiting, diarrhea, depression, and muscle tremors.

Other household items include any medicines, electrical wires, glass, or other breakable items. Christmas trees abound with dangers for both the ever-inquisitive puppy and the adult dog. It is never wise to leave young animals unsupervised in a hostile environment. Even older dogs occasionally get themselves into serious trouble with their keen noses and unquenchable curiosity.

Many plants, even common shrubs, can be toxic to the ever curious dog. This is especially true of puppies whose philosophy dictates: If it doesn't move fast enough, eat it! If you can't get the whole thing in your mouth, chew on it until you can, and if you think someone else is going to get it, swallow it whole.

In any case involving poison, shock, or bites you should call your veterinarian for immediate advice and assistance.

Breeding

Before you start a breeding adventure (and believe me, it is), there are some basic concepts you need to understand. The whole purpose of purebred breeding is to produce dogs that correspond to the written blueprint (standard) of the breed and that will grow up to become healthy companions.

Since breeding your dog could shorten her projected lifespan, make sure this is what you really want and have the time and space to do. Also consider the vast number of dogs produced yearly that do not have homes. Can you place your puppies at eight weeks? If not, do you have adequate space, money, and time to keep them? Research indicates that German Shepherd Dog breeders do not make money on puppies, so if that is your motivation, you may want to reconsider.

Chapter Six

How the German Shepherd Dog Learns

Basic Dogs Versus German Shepherd Dogs

Much of today's training is centered on the rediscovered connection between stimulus/response/reinforcement. However accurate this model is for primary learning, it misses by miles the inherited differences in people and dogs where learning nonsurvival skills is involved. The dog brings to the learning platform a wide variety of genetic variability in desire and abilities along with a deeply ingrained sense of spirit and partnership.

Bred to Bond

Dogs are different from all other animals in that they have been bred for a bonded relationship to man for thousands of years. This selective breeding has brought together some interesting elements. One of the most important would be the love of human contact that promotes strong bonding. These dogs have a great need for approval, often expressed by a desire for tangible reward such

as food, petting, or play activities. Another factor is their great desire to please, which produces a high trainability factor. They are very good at collaboration leading to teamwork. An added bonus is that, in some instances, these dogs exhibit an almost telepathic talent for empathy and response. Often the dog seems to sense what you want before you even ask and may come to you when you are upset without being called. These elements have not been selected to the same degree in all breeds. The German Shepherd Dog, however, seems to be particularly high in all of those special areas. There have been many reported incidents that could be explained only if one considered the possibility of some sort of telepathic interchange.

Unfortunately, no one has yet been able to think of an obedience exercise and have the dog, through only mental response, execute it. However, many anecdotal examples seem to indicate that owners who expect to fail produce a larger number of dogs that do. Owners (handlers) with high expectations more often have dogs that perform at a higher level. There may be many other factors involved, but the bottom line remains that the dog appears to be greatly influenced by the attitude and expectations of the handler.

German Shepherd Dogs are greatly influenced by the moods exhibited by their handlers. They may work with precision but look unhappy if the handler is prone to rough corrections and/or lack of positive communications with the dog. Another downer for the dog lies in the handler's emotional detachment from the dog. Even if positive methods are used and no roughness is involved, the German Shepherd Dog will wilt from lack of emotional feedback much as a flower wilts from lack of moisture.

If a breed has been selected for close bonding, partnership working, and emotional connection, a dog will not flourish when those elements are lacking from the environment. The German Shepherd Dog is a breed apart and should be encouraged to develop all of his vast and rewarding potential.

Bred to Learn

German Shepherd Dogs are basically dogs of great patience. Their extreme desire to please makes them highly receptive to almost any form of training. However, the basic paradigm of stimulus/response/reward, using praise and food as the reward, seems to be the fastest, most efficient, and enjoyable for both dog and handler. This seems to be especially true when used with an attitude of mutual cooperative involvement.

Simply setting the dog up to do the exercises in an emotionally sterile environment often does not produce the happy working dog one is seeking. Research uncovering the dog's specific language and communication skills indicates that using these new tools will both speed learning and make it more enjoyable for all involved.

Because German Shepherd Dogs are bred for a factor known as selective disobedience, there are some slightly different aspects to their training that do not fall cleanly under the

stimulus/response/reward training paradigm. They are a breed apart in many aspects, and it is impractical to attempt to selectively accept or ignore your dog's instincts on the hope that everything will work out okay. It is much safer to develop a set of communications that allows you to tell the dog when he has behaved in a manner that is satisfactory to you, even if you originally gave him a different command. Conversely, you need a command that tells the dog that he was wrong, you were right, and pay more attention next time. These need to be commands, not corrections. This is an advanced level of communication that is difficult to attain, but well worth the effort.

Selecting relevant cues that you want the dog to respond to requires understanding the communication system of the dog. All training must be done operating under the goal of establishing reliable communication, not making obedience a "guessing game" for the dog.

Focus on Communication

Many obedience classes today are still of such a compulsory nature that they are basically unsuited to the eight-week-old puppy. The efforts of some to establish "puppy kindergartens" have been based on random socialization exercises and a little informal and unfocused obedience training. These classes are not aimed at teaching the puppies specific obedience cues with conceptual communication goals.

OPT

The Optimum Placement Technique (OPT) is designed to start any dog at any age and build the training program on a progressive basis until the dog has learned all of the essential foundation exercises and is ready to put them together into trial sequences. OPT is as equally successful with young puppies as with older dogs. This method allows dogs to learn without apprehension or fear

Telling a puppy to do something without showing him first rarely gets the desired response.

of correction while giving the handler time to learn the movements and cues that elicit the correct responses from the dog. OPT allows learning to take place without destroying the human-dog bond that is so essential in the development of an outstanding working-team performance.

The OPT was designed after the author had trained and finished champions, obedience titles (through UD), tracking titles (including German FH), Schutzhund (through III), herding titles through HX, worked with therapy dogs, and trained police and drug dogs. The method has been tested around the world and found to be both efficient and humane. German Shepherd Dogs work exceptionally well due to their extreme trainability, intelligence, and high food drive.

The method of training outlined in this book is as much a philosophy as it is a special way of getting the dog to do what we want him to do. It is based on years of research into the intricacies of the canine learning process.

The results are based on careful observations and testing using a variety of handlers to perform different learning tasks mainly involved with some aspect of canine performance such as conformation, obedience, tracking, herding, and/or Schutzhund competition. Some of the research has been done in America, but it has been augmented by findings from Canada, Australia, Europe, and around the world. The study of learning is an international project as people worldwide work to understand more fully how other species communicate and thus how they learn.

Using this background knowledge, coupled with years of personal experience and experimentation in the field of human learning and animal training, it is my goal to help improve your canine communication skills and establish a rapport that will yield remarkable training results and much personal satisfaction.

One of the first observations of extreme importance to the learning situation is that puppies started between the ages of six weeks and four months learn faster, better, retain learning longer, and learn new skills quicker in later life.

The second most important observation is that food as a primary motivator, when used correctly, develops the most efficient learning techniques.

The third observation is that if the dog is given time to come to the learning situation rather than you placing or acting on him, the dog will retain the exercise longer, do it more willingly, and learn new material better. This involves the process of "learning to learn" that is essential for more complex learning at a later stage.

The fourth concept is that dogs are not verbal, but are capable of learning an extremely large vocabulary of sign and body language. They will eventually develop some abilities in the verbal department, but words that rhyme will nearly always be

interchangeable, thus suggesting that they are truly almost as handicapped with vocabulary skills as we are with scent. However, just as we learn to identify some scent patterns, so dogs can learn and respond to a limited number of verbal cues.

And fifth is the often unrecognized fact that each breed of dog brings to the learning environment more willingness (or innate ability) in some areas than in others. Siberian Huskies bring the drive to pull a sled all day, but they do not exhibit particularly reliable recalls. Retriever breeds are bred to retrieve and give unquestioned response to commands, so they are extremely easy to teach many of the obedience exercises; however, in general, they make very poor protection dogs. Border Collies were bred to watch the sheep, day and night in some cases, and are therefore very attentive and focused when working, making them super candidates for obedience. Most breeds have a specialty that they excel in to the detriment of some of the other canine skills. German Shepherd Dogs were bred with the ideal to be good at a wide variety of jobs. It is often said that they are rarely number one in any area but are second in all. This is a rather broad generalization, but in a good specimen it comes very close.

Chapter Seven

OPT Foundations of Training

Training the Ultimate Puppy

Now you have finished your homework. You have decided on your puppy and communicated this to the breeder. This section will deal with socialization from the puppy level. However, if you have an older dog do not skip this section, for there may be parts in it you need to go back and work through with your dog in order to be assured of the proper foundation for successful future learning.

Research by such noted behaviorists as Scott and Fuller, Dr. Michael Fox, Captain Hulse, and Clarence Pfaffenberger has educated dog trainers on the importance of starting training early. Getting the first response is not the same as training. Training is getting the dog to exhibit the desired behavior the first time (called first response) and then getting the dog to repeat this behavior until reliable and reproducible learning has taken place. There is great variation among German Shepherd Dogs in both this country and abroad that will produce considerable varia-

tion in training time, how much time you have to spend in your training process, and how long you are willing to wait before entering your dog in a competition.

Early obedience trainers in America, such as Hans Toussiti and Blanche Saunders, considered obedience training to be the part of the process that polished the dog for service work or obedience competition. They called the early foundation stage of training "puppy education" and stressed the need to teach the puppy from eight weeks on how to walk on lead, come when called, sit, retrieve, and go out in public for socialization. They encouraged the use of praise and treats and warned against the use of force.

First off, approach your puppy from the angle that he is a canine, not a small furry human. Canines have a slightly different social world that you need to keep in touch with as you enter your relationship. Stanley Coren has some excellent in-depth books on canine communication that summarize much of the current research being done in this field. Through selective breeding, the canine tendency to closely bond with his pack has been extended to include humans. This is a definite plus for us. The other selection has been toward exhibiting either a very neutral reaction to a very strong desire not to hurt members of his own pack, and to protect them against both animal and human invasion. For the first few thousand years the nomadic lifestyles and widely scattered settlements reduced the number of individuals the canine would come in contact with. Most were assumed to be hostile until proven otherwise.

Today we are packed much closer together and the odds are most people entering our territory are non-threatening. Dogs today need more socialization to help them discriminate between friendly strangers and potential threats. They can no longer enjoy the freedom of roaming when living in areas occupied by other "packs" or families.

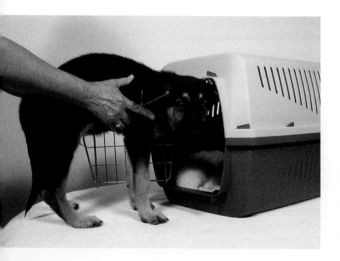

The Crate

It is to be hoped that the breeder has familiarized the puppy with a crate. Put your puppy into the crate that you brought along and let him stay in the crate while you and the breeder finalize the paperwork.

Taking Care of Details

Ideally, papers should have been processed through the AKC by the time the puppies are ready to go to their new home, but delays do occur. Since most reputable breeders will not let puppies go before eight weeks of age, there is sufficient time for all paperwork to have been done. Dogs registered with any other registry, of which there are many privately owned today due to the accessibility of computers, are not eligible to participate in the thousands of AKC events held yearly throughout the United States. They will also be ineligible to compete in any foreign registry, as the AKC is the only internationally recognized registry from this country.

When filling out the AKC registration papers, most breeders will want to fill in the name of the puppy, often including their kennel names. Most trainers want a short, easy-to-say name that is dissimilar from any command words. Pick something that is easy to remember, yet unique. There are books and online sites that offer many suggestions for naming dogs.

Going Home

Finally, your new puppy is in his crate in your car and you have received the registration papers, medical records, pedigree, a picture of the dam and sire of your puppy, your buyer's contract signed by the breeder, and some suggestions on food and proper feeding. Take a deep breath and relax. Take the puppy out of the crate and just sit there and hold him in your arms for at least two minutes, talking and gently stroking him. Then put him back in the crate and go home.

Every 30 minutes to an hour, if the trip is a long one, stop and let the puppy out for a few minutes on lead. If the puppy relieves (himself), praise the performance, using whatever word you intend to use in the future to let him know the time and place to eliminate. I use the word "potty" because it is comfortable for me and I can remember it. It is not important which word or phrase you use so long as you use the same one every time the dog eliminates. This will allow the puppy to know that now is the time and this is the place. Always say "*Good potty*" when the dog relieves himself in an appropriate place. This will be the key to successful housetraining. The dog will find out that there is a place to go that gets your praise. Then, if he makes a mistake in the house and you see it, yell "*No potty*" and instantly take the puppy outside to the proper area.

When you take the puppy outside to relieve himself, stand in one place until he has gone. Praise him, and then walk around if you want to. If you walk around letting him sniff the ground in new places, he will be excited and forget what he is outside for. Then, when he goes back inside, he will remember he needed to go, and he will. This creates a bad situation for the dog.

The puppy will soon understand that it is good to go outside and not good to go inside. This makes for consistent communication with your dog.

One of the most common mistakes made in the housetraining of a puppy is the failure to use the word "*good*" when the dog goes in the appropriate place. If you never let the dog realize there is a right place and all he ever hears is "*No*," all he will learn is that you think he should never go at all. This produces a dog

Talk quietly so he will be recording your voice, confident and comforting, along with the smells of this new home. You can tell the dog, "*Check it out*." Do the same as you go into the house. Your puppy will probably smell around very actively and may repeatedly shy back from strange objects including dark and light spaces in your house that are new and strange. Continue to reinforce this curiosity. If the puppy hangs back, stand still and give him time to look things over. Offer quiet encouragement as he deals with each new experience. This is the foundation for all future encounters. Lay it carefully.

Take your puppy to the place that will be for his food and water. Place the puppy's crate there so he will absorb the smell of his new quarters. Introduce the puppy to each family member one at a time. Nothing can be more disturbing than having several new people cluster around a puppy. It can be overwhelming for any puppy and lead to problems later on when introducing strangers.

The command for meeting new people is "*Make nice*." Tell the puppy to "*Make nice*" as you make introductions to each family member. Have them, one at a time, take the puppy gently and hold him a minute, and then return him to you. After all, you are to be the principal person in his life from now on. You should work to become the person that is always there for guidance and help.

Do not overexert the puppy. After a few minutes of visiting, put him in the crate and let him rest for at least

that, knowing he has to eliminate at the rather regular intervals nature demands, will merely find a place to hide when he relieves himself.

Warning: Another note of warning: Never hit the dog or rub his delicate little tracking nose in any mistakes. Later, when you try to get the puppy to sniff the ground in beginning tracking training, you do not want him remembering that you shoved his nose into something that was extremely distasteful when he was a puppy. Also, fecal matter can do physical damage to the sensitive tissues of the puppy's nose and mouth.

Introducing Puppy to His New Home

At last you arrive home with your new puppy in the crate. Take the puppy out on a lead and walk around the yard for a few minutes.

30 minutes to an hour. Don't forget to take the puppy outside to the prese-lected place for elimination as soon as he wakes up or as soon as you take him out of his crate after any rest period.

All meals will be in the crate for the first few weeks. Anytime you put the puppy in the crate to rest, give him a little chew bone (avoid rawhide treats as they have been found to cause serious problems with some dogs) or a milk bone treat for com-pany. This bonds the puppy to the crate and makes traveling with him to shows or on vacations much eas-ier in the future. As the puppy grows, he will need a larger crate. Most adult German Shepherd Dogs will use either a #400 or #500 airline crate or one of comparable size.

Plan Your Puppy's Future

Use the time while your puppy is resting to review your plans for the future and to go over your notes on how dogs learn and what you are going to work on next. Every minute of the puppy's life will be spent learning. It is your responsibility to ensure that he learns the right things.

There are so many little things a puppy needs to know.

1. He must learn how to ask to go out and then how to get back in again.

2. He must discover what he can and cannot chew, where he is to stay in each room, which room(s) he is to be allowed in, and under what con-ditions he may approach each mem-ber of the family. Many people do not realize how confusing it is to the dog that we will romp and play with him when wearing casual clothes, but protest if he comes near us when we have on dressy clothes.

3. The puppy must learn the rules concerning whether he will be allowed on the furniture, and if so, under what conditions, and he must learn to leave the garbage and other "off-limits" foodstuffs alone.

The list of lessons the puppy will be required to learn is extensive and how you and the dog cope with each one has significant future bearing on his total outlook toward learning and the process of obedience training. How you approach the training of each of the daily matters will influence the overall relationship between you and the dog in all other endeavors.

Consistency

Consistency is the single most important element in the training of any animal. So from now on, you are going to be particularly careful to see that you are consistent with each obedience lesson. Whether training relates to those exercises that will be performed in competition or just to the daily functions of living and inter-acting with the dog around the house and on trips, be consistent.

You must develop the habit of asking yourself, "What do I expect this dog to do in this situation today and one year from now?" Then you want to train toward your answer. You cannot train a dog if you do not have a good grasp of what you expect your dog to be able to do after he has been trained.

All training is done in increments leading up to the finished exercise. Learn to recognize the various steps and reward them as the puppy progresses toward the dog you want him to become. It is unrealistic to ask the puppy to learn the entire obedience routine from the start, just as it would be unrealistic to ask you to learn to play the piano by starting with a difficult recital piece. However, that is exactly what many obedience instructors seem to expect. They start with novice heeling, with the dog sitting on the left side, before the dog even knows how to walk on lead or sit on command.

With the OPT method you will break all exercises down into a number of smaller segments, including several ways to walk on lead, several cues to sit and stand before you combine them into the novice heeling routine. The OPT videos are extremely helpful in organizing your training and checking to make sure you have not left out any important steps along the way.

Housetraining

When your puppy wakes up, you will immediately take him out to potty, remembering always to give the command, "*Potty*," or whatever word you have chosen, and to praise when he complies. You must do this every time in order to firmly establish the word with the deed in the dog's mind. You may miss occasionally, but that will be acceptable so long as you remember to command and praise at every possible opportunity. This is an invaluable lesson for later when you are staying at motels or going to dog shows and the dog must eliminate on command due to the scheduling pressures and the limited availability of suitable places.

Always stand in one place until the puppy has eliminated. After the puppy has pottied, go for a short stroll around the yard, keeping the puppy on a loose lead. A small collar with a plastic snap closure (these are very nice and often adjustable) and a soft 6-foot (1 m) lead are all you need for now. A loose lead is the term used to describe the leash when there is no tension on it. A dog that is pulling you around is said to be on a tight lead. A tight lead also occurs when you are pulling the dog around. To keep a puppy on a loose lead often requires that you follow along with him for a while. In fact, the first two or three times out, it is better if you follow the puppy. Keep the lead loose with plenty of slack and tell the puppy to "*Check it out*." Flexi-Leads are the most wonderful things ever invented for puppy training. Sixteen feet (4.9 m) of lead that doesn't get tangled is absolutely marvelous. If you have never used one, get someone to hold the snap and walk around while you figure out how to stop it and let it out. Training to the Flexi-Lead will make lead training much easier.

Do not take a puppy out without a lead and collar the first few times. You have no control over a dog that is loose, and dogs are quick to take advantage of this situation. Many people are fooled into thinking their puppy is trained because he stays close to them when young, only to find that when the puppy grows up he has no idea about obedience at all and runs away at every opportunity. A mature dog does not feel the need for the safety that a young puppy finds in being near his companion.

Commands

"Good"

At this time you also want to teach the puppy what the word "*Good*" means. The first time the puppy hears "*Good*" the word has no meaning at all, except that the puppy enjoys the sound of your voice. Give the puppy a piece of food (hold the food in the palm of your hand with your hand flat, thus avoiding the puppy learning to grab your hand and fingers when eating, saying "*Good*" as the puppy eats the food). The word "*Good*" will be associated with the eating of the food, which is an enjoyable experience for the puppy. This will give the puppy a positive feeling when he hears the word the next time. That, coupled with your enthusiasm and obvious pleasure, will eventually give the dog

a strong feeling for the word "*Good*." As training progresses, this word alone, in most cases, will be sufficient reward for your dog. German Shepherd Dogs are especially pleased to be praised quietly but sincerely for a job well done. Do not overuse the word by babbling it when there is no reason to be offering the dog a reward. That is the quickest way for "*good*" to lose its positive meaning.

"Let's Go"

As you walk along with the puppy the first few days, keep saying "*Let's go*" each time the puppy starts to move about. You can give gentle tugs on the lead in the direction the puppy intends to go as you give the command, "*Let's go*." You will be pairing a command with a voluntary action for future communication. Anytime you pair or hook something that is known to something that is unknown, the unknown will eventually become known. This is an extremely valuable training device. Dogs learn through a process of chaining new experiences to old ones and expanding their available responses.

After a few days, give the command "*Let's go*" and move in a different direction from where the puppy was headed. Use bits of food if necessary to get the puppy to come your way for the first few times. Praise the puppy, using the word "*Good*" and giving him a bit of food when he comes your way a few steps.

Within three or four days, the puppy will know what "*Let's go*" means and will follow willingly when so commanded. "*Let's go*" is not a heel command. It means that the dog will come along with you on a loose lead, but it is unimportant which side or how far ahead or behind the dog may be. Later you will teach "*Heel*," which is a closer, more accurate positioning on the handler's left side. If you desire to do both AKC-type obedience as well as Schutzhund, you will probably use the command "*Fuss*" for Schutzhund and "*Heel*" for AKC. They are very similar positions, but do have some important differences that the dog is quite capable of learning if properly

instructed. For now, be happy with the puppy following along on a loose lead in the desired direction each time you command, "*Let's go*."

When the puppy has a good grasp of this exercise, you must introduce the concept that this is not an optional exercise. If you say "*Let's go*," and the puppy moves away from you to the end of the lead (and he will do this occasionally), you may give the lead a short quick tug. The tug is an attention getter, not a hard correction. You want just enough of a tug to get the puppy back on the loose lead. Immediately show the food and repeat the "*Let's go*" command. If the dog responds, praise him, using the word "*Good*," and reward him with the food treat.

Do not pull the dog. That can become a game that he will play all day. The snapping action of a short tug on the lead is just unpleasant enough that the puppy will develop the habit of keeping the lead loose as you walk along. Make sure you give no command when you snap the lead. Give the command "*Let's go*," and if there is no response, snap the lead. Repeat the command as soon as the lead is loose and give the praise and reward when the puppy comes along with you.

As you start working the dog toward the left side, you will notice that the position of your hand and the bait has a great deal to do with the dog's position. This is where you really get to participate in the learning process. You must learn to hold the bait in such a way as to keep the dog on the left side and eventually in the correct *heel* position. This may take some time, but you will not be giving the dog any negative learning experiences while you both are learning the *heel* position.

Heel position means that the dog will be on the handler's left side with his neck even with the handler's left leg. Each time you manage to get the dog into the correct *heel* position, you will give the food treat and say "*Good heel.*" No *heel* command is given at this point in the training process; that will come later. You will need several days, even weeks, to become sufficiently skillful to keep the dog in perfect *heel* position for up to 20 to 35 steps. Polishing the *heel* command is generally reserved until the dog is older and more mature. For now, continue to work the dog into the *heel* position and reward a few correct steps with "*Good heel*" and a treat. From this point on, treats are rarely given for "*Let's go,*" but praise can be used occasionally to let the dog know you are pleased with his performance.

The first few days you will probably be able to get the dog in the correct position only three or four times per session. Never jerk the dog when working the heeling exercise. Never say "*No!*" Just keep working the dog until you can maintain position for up to 20 steps between rewards.

The dog must never hear a word in connection with a leash tug at this point in his training. If he does, he will connect that command with the tugging action, not with the desired action that the word should produce. If you jerk a dog and say "*Sit,*" the dog will not learn that the word "*Sit*" indicates a position, but will instead learn that the word "*Sit*" means that he is going to be jerked. The same is true with any word associated with a jerk. Soon the puppy thinks all words mean he is going to get jerked. This leads to much confusion later when you want the dog to sit or lie down and can give only a verbal command. Remember that you are building your training habits at the same time the puppy is learning what you are teaching.

Few handlers are aware of the intricate network of body and situational signals most dogs use to figure out what you want. Later, when the handler cannot give those additional signals but only the word, they are confused when the dog doesn't

respond correctly and often resort to corrections instead of trying to figure out why the dog didn't understand. Separating the command word from all other signals is one of the hardest processes involved in canine communication.

"Make Nice"

Outside walks should be a part of each day's training and should include as many contacts with other people as possible. At each new encounter tell the puppy, "*Make nice*," and then have the person approach and be friendly with you. You may decide to not let your puppy closely socialize with strangers, but he should be willing to be touched and/or petted by anyone you tell him is allowed. Keeping your puppy away from people in order to make him more aggressive when older is a mistake, as this only makes the dog fearful and potentially dangerous. The extent of liability being visited upon negligent and indifferent dog owners is escalating yearly. There is no longer a "first bite" exemption and both fines and jail time are appearing with greater frequency as a result of the behavior of unsocialized dogs.

During your strolls, you will begin to learn all of the wonderful little things that make up your puppy's total personality—how he thinks, how he reacts to dangers (real and imagined), how he relates to the environment, and especially how he reacts to anything new or different. Bonding is an ongoing process that can be enhanced if you take the time to stroke your puppy and say a few words of comfort or assurance when he encounters problems along the way.

Dogs can sense an honest compliment, even if it is only a slight touch of the hand. Likewise, they can tell if a person is trying to "lay it on" and are insincere. Some dogs do not seem to care but most German Shepherd Dogs do. Your dog needs to trust you and, even more important, you must have some trust and faith in your dog. If you are insecure and unsupportive, you may find that later, when the dog is up against a hard situation or a difficult task, he may falter at just the wrong moment and fail you when otherwise he could have succeeded.

The necessity to be supportive is especially apparent when a difficult tracking course is encountered. More often than not, the dog fails because of lack of support and/or trust from the handler rather than from his inability to perform. So now, while your puppy is young and impressionable, let him know you have confidence in him and will offer support as he overcomes the many problems that will be encountered along the way.

This may seem trivial now, but it is not. You and your puppy are developing patterns of learning and coping together. If you are harsh and punitive, if you lack patience and understanding, and in general do not support your puppy, your dog's performance in the future will reflect the effects of this interaction in a magnified form. However, if you develop patience and understanding, and if you let the puppy know it is all right to check things out and that you are there if he needs you, your dog will grow confident and secure.

"Fear-of-Failure" Syndrome

Present each new learning experience in a positive manner that will be easy for the young dog to learn, and you will have an adult dog that can face each new challenge with strength, determination, and confidence. Your puppy must come to know he has a partner to trust who will back him up when needed. Another benefit from this type of approach is that it produces a dog that is not afraid to try new things for fear of reprisal should he fail. It is worth noting that dogs can develop the "fear-of-failure" syndrome seen in many people if they are discouraged sufficiently when attempting to learn new things.

"Phooey"

While this is going on outside during part of the day, you will also be working inside on simple exercises that lay the foundation for all of the obedience training that is to come. Sit on the floor with the puppy and show him a bit of food. You may

have to let the puppy eat a piece or two from your hand to learn what it is. This is also the point at which he learns to take food from your hand without eating fingers. If the puppy attacks the food and gets part of you in the process, say, "*Phooey*," and hold your hand flat against the floor with the food in the palm. Praise your puppy for taking the food and not biting you. Gradually hold your hand higher off the floor and over a period of time move the food from your palm to where you can hold it in your fingers. Teaching discrimination in biting and wolfing food at this point in the training can eliminate the necessity of harsh corrections later.

"Find it—Here"

Next, take a small piece of food, show it to the puppy, and then toss the food out a few inches in front of him on the floor. It may take a time or two for the puppy to see it, but when he does and moves toward the food, give the command "*Find it*."

As soon as the puppy has eaten the food, call, "*Here*," and hold your hand down with a bit of food on your palm where the puppy can see it. The puppy will come running back to your extended hand for the food. This is the "*Find it—Here*" exercise, which forms the foundation for much of the future training. Repeat this exercise as often as possible. Let any other family members that you want the dog to bond with practice the "*Find it—Here*." Never let any stranger or person you do not want the dog to bond with do this exercise with your dog.

The "*Find it—Here*" is the basis for many OPT–trained exercises, including both the formal and informal recall, the straight front sit on recall, the retrieves, and the "*Go outs*" in both Schutzhund and obedience exercises. It is also a superb bonding exercise and the exercise that helps teach the dog to find each member of the family by name. The more the dog bonds to you, the easier and more enjoyable your future training will be. This exercise can be done on lead the first few times and is especially helpful in teaching the dog that the lead is a means of communicating rather than punishing. When the puppy gets good enough to go out several feet to the food, give a couple of gentle tugs just before the recall. This helps associate gentle tugs with moving in a desired direction. As soon as the puppy catches on, do this exercise both in the house and outside. Also do as many off lead as possible. This lays the foundation for the dog to return to you when called regardless of whether there is a lead on or not.

As you go for your walks both on and off lead at this stage, bend down occasionally and call the puppy to you with the command "*Here*." Position your hand on a level with the puppy's nose and hold your palm open to him with the food readily visible. When the puppy comes, let him have the food and say "*Good*" as he is eating. Then give the dog two pats on his left side then let him go out to play and explore again. From this point on, each time you finish an exercise, you will give the dog two (not three or six) pats on his left side. This is the same as saying, "*Okay, you're through*." This physical contact does a much better job of communicating that message over a period of time than does a verbal command.

The Two-Pat Release

The "*two-pat release*," as it is called, will be especially helpful in the future with stays, tracking, and protection or bite work. The two-pat release communicates to the dog that he is done for now and/or that the exercise is over. When doing these recalls, do not use the word "*come*." "*Come*" is a strictly formal recall to be used later in competition obedience exercises where several basic exercises will be combined to make one performance exercise. "*Here*" is the foundation for "*Come*" and will remain the informal command to get the dog in your general vicinity where you just want to touch, catch, or play with him. "*Here*" is the word used for all daily recalls and will be used later in combination with other basic words to establish new command words for specific competition exercises.

Have Your Own Search and Rescue Dog

Many families experience the tragedy of losing a family member— no, really, losing one—not being able to find their location at that particular time. People can wander away, fall, or become injured and be unable to respond when called, be lost in many ways that are beyond their control. Nearly every family has a live-in people finder—their dog. Any breed of dog from four months and older can use that incredible nose to help locate or indicate either where they are or where they are not within the limits of the dog's environment and training.

Once the dog is reliable on the "*Find-It*" and "*Here*," you can train the dog to find any member of your family by name and/or scent. Tell the dog to "*Find*" (family member name). Have that person hold a hand out with food and call the dog "*Here*." The target person then tells the dog to find the family member who sent him and holds the food out and gives the command "*Here.*" Send the dog back and forth between the targets, getting greater distance until you finally are working out-of-sight finds. Use the entire house and any surrounding areas where the dog is allowed to go.

Once the dog has figured out this exercise, start adding other family members one at a time until the dog can find any family member by name. Some members may be too small or unable to interact with the dog. Add these members after the dog understands the concept of "*Find*" in relation to people. With those targets, you have the dog go to them and receive a reward from you. Eventually, you can train the

dog to find the target person, return to you, and lead you back to the target or sit by the target until you come reward him. This is especially useful with very small children and older or handicapped adults.

Most dogs trained this way are fairly reliable at moderate distances. You can also give the dog the scent from some article and pair that with the person's name until he can work it either way. Using a scent pattern will make him more reliable over a longer period of time and distance.

Most dogs have a high to normal energy level and thrive on having a job to do. This is an informal exercise that bonds the dog to all members of the family and can offer a great deal of personal comfort if a family member ever gets out of sight.

"*See It*"

If you want the dog to go in a specific direction, you must first get him to focus on that direction. As you practice the "*Find it—Here*," you can eventually teach the puppy to look at the food using the command "See it" before letting him go after the treat. This will be the foundation for the "Go outs" in both Schutzhund and AKC utility work. A dog tends to go in the direction he is looking, so if you can teach him to look, on command, in the direction you want him to go, you will maximize your chances of good straight "*Go outs*" and great jumps in the future. Eventually the command "*Away*" will chain several basic actions, including the "*Go out*," to produce the competition exercise. Eventually, the dog must, from a moving *heel*, go straight away from the handler on command for a distance of up to 50 yards and then execute another command. Getting the dog to go away briskly in a straight line for the desired distance can be difficult without a good foundation.

Aside from the advantages this exercise gives in competition, it is a great way to get the dog away from you when needed. If you are engaged in some activity (lawn mowing is a good example) and want the dog to go away, this is the foundation. You can add a positional command later. Then you can send your dog to a specific spot and have him stay there in whatever position you tell him until you are ready for him to move. This type of communication has a variety of uses throughout the dog's life. Most of the exercises taught in the OPT foundation are as useful in daily living as they are for the purposes of competition.

Jumping

The "*Find it*" is very useful, not only in training the "*Go out*," but also for jumping. Starting with young puppies is easy and fun. Use a hula-hoop. Place the bottom on the ground and hold the top in one hand. Flip the food through the hoop and send the puppy on a "*Find it*." If the puppy tries to go around the hoop, swivel it as the puppy moves so the puppy must go through to get the food. Do not raise the hoop more than an inch or two until the puppy is old enough to jump as high as his chest. This teaches the concept to go through and over something that he could go around or under. Once the dog accepts this concept, jump training is much easier and more reliable.

The Nose-Lift Sit

Another exercise you want to start at the same time is "*Sit*." This is a very important foundation exercise for both heeling and straight fronts. You have probably noticed that when a dog looks up for any length of time, he will sit. The action of looking up puts a strain on the dog's neck that he wishes to relieve. Dogs are rather curious animals, so when we talk, the

dog tends to look up at us to see where the noise is coming from. As he looks up, his neck becomes tired, so he will sit to straighten out his spine. If you happen to be saying "*Sit, sit, sit*" at the time, you may be led to believe that the dog is sitting on command, when, in fact, he is not. In OPT training you never give a verbal command for an exercise the dog does not already know, because if you do and the dog does not obey, then you will be forced to make him obey, thus setting up an unpleasant chain of responses in the dog's mind.

You need to get the puppy to sit, without touching him or using any force, so you can pair the word "*Sit*" with the actual act of sitting. The easiest way to do this, and keep your mouth shut at the same time, is with food. Do not give the command to sit and do not touch the puppy. Just take a small piece of food and hold it close to the puppy's nose. The puppy will smell it and make motions to get it. Hold the food close to his nose but in your fingers so he can't get it, then move the food back and up so the puppy's nose points to the ceiling. You will have to hold the food securely in your fingers, close to the puppy's nose, and you may have to try this a time or two to get the correct response. When the puppy's nose is pointing to the ceiling he will sit to relieve the strain. Give him the food and say, "*Good sit.*" Repeat the "*Good sit*" while the puppy is still sitting. The puppy is hearing the word "*Sit*" while he is in the sitting position. There is no stress, and there are no other variables to interfere with the puppy learning the word.

Since the puppy has heard "*Good*" with several other exercises and it was always paired with eating food, he is getting a good feeling about sitting. This is called pairing or chaining. You chain the word "*Good*" with a primary reinforcer such as food until the word "*Good*" becomes a secondary reinforcer by taking on all of the good sensations that were produced by the primary reinforcer— food. Eventually, the word "*good*" will be as rewarding to the dog as the food was in the beginning.

This exercise is called the *nose-lift sit* and is the first response exercise for all future types of sitting. Practice *nose-lift sits* as often as you can during the first weeks of training. Remember to give no command—

just get the dog into a sitting position by lifting his nose with the food. Then say "*Good, sit,*" give the food, and release with the two pats on his left side.

"Stand"

While working on the *nose-lift sit*, you can also work in a few "*stands.*" Teaching the two at the same time avoids confusion later when the dog is asked to sit, down, and stand on a verbal command while moving at heel. Using the same approach as with the *sit*, catch the dog's nose with the food scent. As soon as the puppy smells the food, he will stop. Now you are going to learn about the mechanics of the dog's body. If you hold the food too high, the dog will sit. In order to get a *stand*, you must keep the dog's nose at the same level as his topline. Once the dog stops and stands, give the food and say "*Good stand.*" After the puppy settles down, try to move the food away from the nose an inch or two without the puppy moving. Short in-and-out motions seem to work best at this stage. If you can get the food an inch away and back before the puppy moves, give the treat and say "*Good stand.*" Don't forget the two-pat release before he moves. Work toward being able to hold the puppy in a *stand* for two or three seconds with the food a few inches away. That is about all that is needed at this stage of the training to start setting up this foundation exercise.

The Nose-Drop Down

The *down* is also an important foundation exercise that should be started as soon as the puppy can do a reliable *nose-lift sit*. From the sitting position, catch the puppy's nose with the food. Bring the food down to a point directly between the puppy's front feet, then out along the floor until the puppy is in a *down* position. Say "*Good down*" and give the treat. Do a *two-pat release* after each exercise.

Do not worry if you occasionally fail to remember to give the pats. As time goes on, giving the *two-pat release* will become an automatic reflex for you each time you give the dog a command that he executes correctly. Just as the dog is chaining your various body signals to rewarded responses, you will be learning the

sequence of cue, response, praise, reward, two-pat release. Do not mistake the *two-pat release* with petting. When you are playing with your dog in an informal relaxed manner, you can pat him anywhere and as often as you desire. Such affectionate contact is a super way to relax, but it has nothing to do with the above study sessions. Love is a personal, spontaneous sharing of emotions between you and your dog. Praise is a formal routine that is built into the study sessions in a very stylized manner.

Corrections

There may be times during training when corrections are necessary, but there are very few problems that cannot be solved with additional training. A correction is given only after a dog knows something and refuses to do it. If you give two corrections for an error and get no improvement, you can be assured that the fault lies not with the dog's disobedience but with his lack of total understanding. A cue is missing or the total process of internalizing the cue/response is not complete. Also, like people, dogs do forget and they do simply make mistakes. Allow for this in your training.

Discipline Versus Punishment

Punishment generally occurs when the dog is doing something dangerous and refuses to stop on the *"That will do,"* *"Phooey,"* or *"Make nice"* commands. This covers such incidents as fighting, chasing cars or animals, biting kids, and any truly dangerous activity. The severity of the punishment, from a harsh word on, is dictated by the seriousness of the offense.

Discipline is what your teaching and training should accomplish. Like soldiers, there is a way of life that is socially acceptable and dictated by the people and environment in which living takes place. It involves things that have to be done and things that are done simply because that is the way they need to be done.

Avoid corrections, restrict punishment to absolutely necessary events, and train for discipline until it is an accepted and enjoyed way of life.

Bite and Release Foundations

Another aspect of this early training will include the foundation for both the biting and the *"Out"* or letting go when told. This is a super safety factor that should be taught to all dogs. Accidents can happen. All dogs can "turn on" (bark aggressively) or bite something or someone under certain conditions. Turning one off, or getting him to release or stop barking on command, could be essential at some time in the future.

Use a small piece of burlap rag to get the puppy biting on something that is moving. Play with it, teasing the puppy by dragging the burlap along the floor. As soon as he gets it, let go the first few times. As the dog gets more enthusiastic, hold on and offer a little resistance. Give him a little fight, but keep the struggle in proportion to the size of the dog and the tenderness of his teeth. Always let him win before he gets tired or discouraged. As soon as the dog gets to the point where he attacks the burlap and takes a firm bite, you will start laying the foundation for the "*Out*" or release. As with all other exercises, no command is given. Once the dog has the burlap and is holding on tightly, let go of it. Slip a couple of fingers under the collar where it crosses the back of the neck. Gently lift up until the front feet are a few inches off the floor. Do this gently. The dog will probably fling the sack back and forth a time or two and then go still. Within a few seconds the mouth will open and the burlap will fall out. Do not touch the burlap at any time during this operation. As soon as the burlap falls to the floor, say "*Good out*," let the dog down immediately, pick up the burlap, give a short struggle, and let the dog win. Do this only once or twice in each session. Keep these sessions short so the dog will not get tired and want to quit. Starting the *Out* in this manner makes for extremely smooth and reliable releases in advanced Schutzhund training and never seems to lessen the dog's strength of attack.

The safety feature of this exercise lies in the fact that if your dog ever gets something in his mouth you want out undamaged, the collar lift and the command "*Out*" will do the job. Remember to keep your hands off whatever the dog has in his mouth; otherwise, it will become another game of tug of war.

The first indication that your German Shepherd Dog has that essential inbred quality for protection will come one day when he "alerts" (same as "turns on") on one of your friends, neighbors, or a stranger. This can happen anywhere from 10 weeks to 14 months of age and is characterized by barking in a challenging manner. Your first thought will probably be to make him stop. You may realize immediately that this is not a stranger or a threat and you do not want the puppy to grow up to be an uncontrollable biter. However, stopping the alert immediately at this point could cause many training problems later as the puppy or young dog might learn that you consider it undesirable to bark at people at all.

Friend Versus Foe

The untrained dog cannot make an accurate discrimination between who is good and who is not. One of the major goals of all training that involves dogs with the potential to eventually bite someone is to develop the correct discrimination of who is fair game and who is not, and under what circumstances these rules hold true.

This is a German Shepherd Dog, bred to protect. Protect on some

that is lower and more intense than you normally would.

As soon as the puppy understands that you are pleased with this action, you give the command *"Enough"* and/or *"That will do."* If the puppy does not stop barking, repeat the command, let him have some slack on the lead (but do not turn him loose), and tell him to *"Make nice"* (the command he has been learning that means "Be friends"). Walk up to the person and talk in a friendly manner. Keep the dog under control for safety's sake, but most dogs, especially young puppies, will immediately relax and follow your lead. As soon as the puppy is comfortable, repeat the command *"Make nice,"* and have the person pat the puppy. If the puppy tries to jump up, lower the lead and stand on it so that when he attempts to go up, the lead will jerk him down. This is a self-correction exercise and very effective when dogs want to jump up for any reason. Reward and praise the dog when he stops jumping.

Each person must make a decision regarding the extent to which the dog will be allowed or encouraged to "alert." It is slightly more difficult to teach the dog to bark at noises in the night that might be important to your well-being and not end up keeping you awake all night "alerting" on every leaf that falls or every car that passes on the street. It is much easier to teach this to the dog that lives in a quiet neighborhood or in the country than it is to teach the urban dog. However, it is an equally important

occasions means bite. Whether the dog is a home or competition dog, he should be trained to discriminate between friendly, nonthreatening people and potential threats. It is not necessary to ever let the dog actually bite during this training unless you intend to do Schutzhund competition.

Step one in this training sequence is to gain control of the dog by holding the collar or lead and praising the dog with a specific word that will be used later to elicit the bark response. Avoid cutesy words like *"kill"* or *"get 'em,"* as they could get you into serious legal trouble later. Either the word *"Search"* or the German command of *"Pass auf"* (watch or speak) is quite acceptable and can later be tied into the Schutzhund protection exercises very successfully. Tell the dog to *"Search"* and praise him for barking. If that is too formal for you, ask the dog, *"What is it?"* Use a tone exercise if you want the full value of the dog's abilities.

Developing Your Dog's Talents

As your dog matures, keep working with his talents as they develop. This will take many months, because you must investigate every noise your dog barks at for the first month or so. You have to reward the dog on the correct ones and tell him that you are not really interested in the affairs of the neighbor's cat and other such trivial incidents enough times for him to start making a difference. Dogs adjust to routines rather quickly, so it will not take the puppy too long to recognize such normal disturbances as the garbage man, the people next door on their way to work, or any regular nonthreatening noises and events that occur along the street. But, he should always alert you to anyone who invades the space you deem yours around or in your house, regardless of the hour.

As the puppy matures, arrange to have some of your friends drop by at odd hours and make noises so you can have the opportunity to praise the puppy for being on guard and sounding the warning. This will balance the times you let the dog know you were not interested in a particular incident. Remember to praise the correct "alert," give the appropriate command such as "*Search*," and then stop the dog with the command

"*Enough*." If your dog does not bark at the things that you want him to, you may have to help him along. To aid the dog in identifying a potential threat, use such questions as "*Who's there?*" or "*What's that?*" in an excited tone when you are sure that a person is outside. Later, if you suspect something, you can alert the dog with these questions and elicit a more intense response. Use a low but excited tone of voice for these questions. This will help later in your training if you start formal protection.

Many excellent daytime watchdogs will sleep soundly through a break-in and burglary if it occurs between the hours of midnight and six in the morning. They have been thoroughly trained to ignore anything that happens during these hours, and they have learned that when you go to bed, you will take over responsibility for all protection and alerts until the morning. This sounds stupid to us, but it is perfectly logical to the dog that has been told to "*Shut up and go to sleep*" during all of the nighttime hours of his life.

Thus, starting with the young puppy, investigate any noise that starts him barking. Reinforce the response to the noises you want to hear about and discourage those you would rather not. Above all, do not discourage the dog from barking at people coming into the house after you go to bed. You will get accustomed to the routine of quietly praising your dog and then turning him off with the "*Enough*" command. Eventually you will have a comforting feeling in the knowledge that nobody—family or otherwise—is going to be able to sneak up on you while you are asleep. You may adjust your personal training to let the dog ignore family members, but remember, what you teach the dog is exactly what he will do.

Chewing

Anytime the puppy wants to chew on things you do not want chewed on, either give the puppy a little play with the burlap or give him an acceptable toy or chew bone. It is permissible to say *"Phooey"* as you gently remove the puppy from chewing on the undesirable object; however, yelling *"No"* each time the puppy does something you consider undesirable has been found to be

counterproductive in later training. The use of *"No"* spoken either loudly or harshly should be reserved for forbidden behavior, such as biting you or any member of the family, or stealing food from the table. *"No"* is a forever word and means the dog must never do whatever he is being reprimanded for. *"No"* must not be used to stop the dog from doing something that you may want him to do later. Also, the overuse of *"No"* tends to destroy its effectiveness and the dog will soon lose respect and simply ignore it. The most efficient results will be gained from simply stopping the dog from whatever he is doing with the gentle, but firm, reprimand of *"Phooey"* and placing him in a position to do something that is acceptable. If you tire of this game before the puppy does, put him in the crate or out in the exercise pen for a while, and let both of you rest.

Don't Bite the Hand That Feeds You

Every day admit your puppy to the family circle to work on "general etiquette." While playing with you or some member of your family, the puppy may start exerting the full influence of those needle-sharp puppy teeth. Your first reaction is to give the puppy a whack and let him know you are not going to stand for that. Stop and think. If you use your hand, it might destroy confidence in the all-powerful goodness of you, and the dog could easily become hand-shy. If you use any other item, that will pair the other item in his mind with something unpleasant. This type of accidental pairing can lead to future problems. If you use a rolled-up newspaper, as many people do, your dog may associate the newspaper with any stranger who delivers your paper. The dog will not accept a potential beating from a stranger. In a dog's mind, you as the pack leader, have the right to punish him, but he will not permit others the same privilege.

If you strike your dog with a stick, what will happen when the decoy threatens him with a stick in the advanced Schutzhund exercises? Will he let go of the sleeve because he associates being corrected for biting with a stick hit when he was a very impressionable puppy? Many a potentially super Schutzhund prospect has been ruined in early life by being systematically taught to never bite anything or anyone. This is extremely difficult conditioning to overcome in an adult dog.

Obviously, you cannot allow the puppy to bite you and your family, even in play, so you must find another way to let him know his actions are unacceptable without stifling his potential. In all training, it is better to first teach the dog to do something you approve of that is counter to whatever you do not want the dog to do. Biting is no different. Go back to the burlap rag, only now you are going to use it to focus the biting and reinforce the concept that

there is a time and a place to bite as well as a command to stop.

When your puppy nibbles at you, gently remove his mouth and encourage him to bite the burlap rag. Use the collar lift to cause the dog to drop the object. Now you can communicate to the dog that biting is allowed, but still have an *"Out"* and *"Enough"* command to use if he bites you. Naturally, there will be an occasional dog that will not learn this lesson easily. So, there is a plan B. When you observe mother and father dogs raising a litter (which we do as often as possible because of the numerous positive benefits involved), you will see the various ways they correct and train their puppies. Sometimes a puppy will try to nurse after he is weaned, or, heaven forbid, try to take a bone or piece of food from the father. Even overstepping the bounds of the puppy's authority in the presence of an adult dog will often bring down the wrath of the offended individual. Nearly every one of these corrections is the same. They are simple and extremely effective. The adult bites the young offender on the muzzle, gently at first, for minor offenses, harder for serious or second offenses. Often puppies go screaming and wetting across the floor after an especially severe (and nearly always well-deserved) correction. However, I have never seen the skin broken, and have never seen a puppy that did not return, ask forgiveness, and seem to adore the adult more than he did before the corrective incident.

Okay, I can hear you saying, "I am not about to bite my dog on his nose." And, as a matter of fact, I am not especially fond of dog hair in my mouth either. Actually, several of the noted wolf researchers do just exactly that, but I have found a suitable substitute method. It works, and it keeps all that dog hair off your tonsils. We will let the puppy's sharp little teeth do the job for us.

Grasp the muzzle with your left hand and roll the lips into the mouth, pressing them hard against the upper teeth until the desired results are achieved (a short yip of pain). At the same time say "*Phooey!*" Having handled the puppy in a manner that he understands inherently and for which he has generations of built-in acceptance, you will achieve the desired communication. If you are observant and place your hand in such a manner that it obscures the puppy's vision before you apply pressure, you will find he never becomes hand-shy. All of the dogs we have corrected and seen corrected in this manner have never shied on a "*Stay*" hand signal or when you extend your hand to pet them.

This is a special correction, reserved only for biting you and/or immediate members of your family and for stealing food from the table. This is probably one of the neatest, most efficient, and handiest corrections you can ever master. Pair the word "*Phooey*" with it when the puppy is young and you will have a super command to let the dog know when you do not approve of some-

thing in the future. This should not be used with older dogs as they have passed from the puppy acceptance age and into the independent age where they might be more than willing to challenge your authority.

Biting Strangers

Biting strangers is a delicate matter. The best way to avoid future training problems is to not let your puppy get in a situation that might lead to problems. Strangers do not need to touch your dog unless you tell the dog and the stranger that it is permissible. Remember the command "*Make nice.*" You must also be willing to take time to monitor the puppy's playtime with family members until the puppy learns the ropes. The "*Find it—Here*" and other obedience exercises will make this much easier. Eventually, the dog should bond to both you and all of the important members of your family sufficiently to not want to bite them.

If a nonfamily member insists upon doing something to a dog that would cause him to bite, either remove the dog from this intolerable situation or be prepared to praise the dog and explain to the person why you are not correcting him.

Note: There is one exception to all rules, and it involves babies and small children. No puppy or dog should ever be allowed to endanger them. Most dogs, if introduced properly and trained over a period of time, will accept children for what they are and not bother them. If the dog will not, then you will be responsible to see that the dog stays away from the children (and the children stay away from the dog) so that no damage can occur. Some dogs simply do not like children. It is rather rare, but when you recognize it, it then becomes your responsibility to take appropriate safety measures.

You want to retain the dog's spirit. You want to preserve your dog's independence and courage, yet still earn respect and devotion. Control is essential, but be careful not to overdo it with a young puppy as it could cause you a great deal of trouble in the future.

"*Make nice*" is the first connection the dog gets with the concept to not bite or become aggressive with the object (person or animal) of your interest. The *stand for examination* in obedience and conformation provides an excellent use for this command. It releases the dog from the necessity of protecting you from strangers who often are making you nervous. The dog cannot distinguish one form (social) of fear from another (physical).

Once the dog has a good handle on the concept of "*Make nice*," it helps build confidence, teach discrimination, and extends the dog's horizons into friendly water. Other exercises will help develop keys to his understanding of when it is acceptable to exhibit aggression. Both in daily life and on a training field, the dog can learn the signals of aggression, your response to them,

and the response you expect of him in return.

We All Need a Little Space

All dogs need an outside exercise pen that is spacious enough to move around in and that is fitted with some type of shelter from the sun, wind, and rain. The exercise area should not be the entire yard unless the yard is completely free of any type of vegetation or objects that you want to preserve. If a dog is allowed free run in an area containing property subject to destruction, the puppy will probably learn to destroy it. A puppy has a very active drive to investigate the environment and, from his point of view, the best way to check it out is to sniff it, and then go to work on it with paws and mouth. A puppy will not understand why you are angry if you scream at him because he dug up the flowers, and he will definitely be upset if you strike him for doing so. The only lessons your dog will learn from such experiences are that you are erratic, unpredictable, given to fits of violence, and should be watched with extreme caution anytime you approach when he is outside. A puppy will not connect scolding or punishment with what he has done. You can easily see the result of this type of behavior when you begin working outside with the lead removed (off lead).

If the puppy suspects you are upset, he may be tempted to leave the scene, especially if he remembers anything unpleasant that has happened to him in the past.

So make sure that the puppy is given a safe place to play outside so he will not have to wait in the crate for long periods of time when you cannot supervise or provide company. Have some type of dry shelter in the area so your puppy can escape from the elements when necessary, and always keep fresh water within reach. Dogs can last much longer without food than they can without water.

Don't Jump on Me Unless I Invite You

Somewhere between two and four months of age most dogs decide that jumping up on you is a great way to say hello. There are two approaches to this problem: Jump up on command or never jump up. If you want the dog to jump up on command, hold your left arm out and low enough for the puppy to put his front feet over it. Give the command you want to use, pat your arm, then help the puppy get his front feet over your arm. Praise the puppy, give the *two-pat release*, and command "*Off.*" Stand up. The puppy will be off your arm. Do that a few times to give the puppy a chance to realize that coming up is to be on the arm and is only allowed when told.

To teach the puppy not to jump on people when meeting, attach a

4-foot (1.2 m) light line (or drop the leash) and simply stand on it. Give the puppy just enough slack to jump, but not far enough to get up on you. Don't say anything. Do a *nose-lift sit*, reach over, and pet the puppy. This also works on adult dogs. If you have a persistent jumper, let him drag the line around and meet lots of people. The sequence is step on line, have the person approach, wait quietly until the puppy settles (generally he will sit on his own), then pet and reward the puppy in the *sit*. Works like a charm.

You can also use this technique to keep the puppy on the floor by you when eating or watching television. With the leash and dragline on, take the lead and start for the door. If the puppy forges ahead, step on the dragline. As soon as the puppy is stopping before dashing out the door, remove the lead and practice some more. Keep the dragline on as a safety line. This avoids the "lead-dependent" dog who still runs through the door when the lead is removed.

Play Retrieving

Play retrieving is an excellent exercise for both you and your puppy. Roll a ball across in front of your puppy. Most will immediately take chase. Some will pick it up and start dancing around. A few will bring it straight back to you. If yours doesn't, put a dragline on him so he can't run away. When he gets the ball, give

a "*Here*" command and work the puppy back to you until you can get the ball. Give a treat and toss it again. Don't do too many per session so interest will stay high. This is not a substitute for the formal retrieve later, but is lots of fun for both you and your dog. Do not use any formal obedience commands during this playtime activity. Select other words that do not duplicate or sound like those you will use later.

Some German Shepherd Dogs make passable Frisbee dogs, but be extremely careful about the jumping up and coming down. They can sustain serious injuries if they fall the wrong way while young bones are still growing.

If you are going into any type of competition or simply want to expand your puppy's education as he matures, read the following chapters and select the exercises you feel ready to add to your puppy's curriculum. Most advanced exercises can be started prior to four months, but many cannot be completed until the dog is more mature, both mentally and physically.

Chapter Eight

Obedience

Introduction

If you have completed the puppy training section, you are now ready for a more thorough foundation in canine communication. If you started with an older dog, go back and review the puppy section, making sure that the dog has covered all of the preparation exercises.

Rules for competition can be obtained from AKC or other performance-oriented organizations by writing or going online (see Appendix A for addresses). A thorough knowledge of the rules avoids point loss through preventable mistakes.

Foundation work is essential. Research indicates that dogs that work out of fear rather than through teaching and practice rarely make happy, cooperative partners. Circus dogs that must perform reliably two or three times a day over a period of years are trained with teaching and practice, and nearly all of the more successful animal trainers use food as the primary motivator and reinforcer.

Food

The first step is to use the food to get the dog into the proper position.

Food will enable you to get the primary response with patience and no pain. Immediately reinforce the correct performance with food and praise. If you do this a sufficient number of times, the dog will learn what is expected of him. Later, the food will be partially phased out through variable reinforcement and almost completely replaced with the secondary reinforcer, "*Good*." A keen insight into the way a dog learns, plus practice and relearning when problems develop, are the key ingredients that make most professional performers so successful.

Practice

Efficient practice is the key to success in performance. Work smoothly to develop reliability. If your dog has the capacity to be fast, then time, practice, and confidence will allow that capacity to develop. Speed in any exercise is the result of repetition and confidence plus motivation and ability. Nearly all dogs and most people go much slower than normal when learning anything. Give yourself and the dog ample time to learn before applying any pressure for speed.

In competition, a dog that is accurate and reliable, although a little slow, will win more often than one that is fast and inaccurate. Many of the top-scoring obedience dogs have very high failure rates. They fail with speed and class, but they do fail. If you want a dog to save your life in some future situation, you might want to cultivate the accuracy and reliability factor first. All the flash in the world is worthless if the dog fails to give the correct response when it is really needed.

The AKC, as well as several other organizations, offers a variety of obedience and performance competitions. Obtain a rulebook to determine specific requirements and guidelines for entering and competing for titles and degrees.

Most beginning degrees require that the dog move on the handler's left side on a loose lead or off lead over a designated course. The dog will make turns, change pace, and halt in place. There will be *recall*, *sit*, *down*, and *stand* commands under varying conditions. In the advanced levels the dog will retrieve on the flat and over a jump as well as jumping hurdles on command. Hand signal exercises and both directed and scent discrimination retrieves are also incorporated at the advanced levels.

Training for competition builds on the foundation training with the puppy. Going to matches and licensed trials are excellent ways to get insights and experience about dog shows in general and obedience events in particular.

General Advice

Using the conformation show ring to socialize and condition your dog is highly recommended. Since most conformation shows require only that the dog move about the ring on lead and stand reasonably still for an examination, this is the easiest competition to start showing the dog.

In the conformation ring, you can stay close to your dog, encourage him, talk to him, and reward him—a very positive experience for the dog.

Even if you are not planning on future conformation competition, this socialization helps produce a dog that will "*make nice*" on command and permit future judges, your veterinarian, or a friend to pet him.

Puppy matches offer excellent training experiences and give you a chance to teach your dog that people should not be bitten without cause, that many people are very nice, and examination by strangers is allowed when you signal approval. This type of exposure between the ages of four months and a year will help stabilize your dog's personality and make him far more acceptable in everyday society. It is best for a dog to learn while young to cope with crowds, noise, and the process of traveling and crating, to relieve himself when and where told, and to function amid the distracting presence of other dogs.

Show dog people are thoroughly accustomed to dogs, especially rambunctious puppies, and will offer understanding and supportive help at a time when it is most important. You will also get some evaluations as to the good and bad points of your dog in relationship to the standard of your breed. If you ever intend to breed your dog, it will help you in making the selection of a breeding partner that will be strong in the areas in which your dog may be weak.

There is one important point to be stressed concerning the German Shepherd Dog. This is a breed that was bred to be a protection dog. Your dog cannot protect you if he is home in the run or crate or if he has to be tied up securely when you are in public or have company. If you do not make a friend, companion, and partner of your dog, you are not giving his natural protective instincts scope to develop. Discrimination is the key to successful utilization of a good Schutzhund or protection dog. Many dogs know how to bite, but the really useful dog also knows when not to bite.

All of these exercises in the OPT foundation series are designed for safe and reliable home communication as well as setting the dog up for future competition. See the Appendix for OPT videos and DVDs for additional information on both the foundation and advanced obedience training.

Training time varies from dog to dog. The general rule of thumb is that it takes about 200 repeats of any single exercise before the dog actually knows it. Some individua

dogs may take more than 200 repeats, some less.

The Leash

A few concepts about leashes need to be addressed at the beginning. The dog hooks everything in his environment to learning. The leash is a very visible part of the environment. If you train with the leash in your hand, it will make a huge difference in the dog's performance when you have to remove it. Therefore, it is much more desirable to train the dog without the leash being visible. The most efficient way to do this, and still retain some control over the dog, is to drop the leash on the ground and stand on it. Throughout all the following exercises, with the exception of the "*Let's go*," the leash should be on the ground.

Learning to step on and off the leash may take some practice on your part, but it will be well worth the effort in the long run. Dogs simply do not pay attention to things that are dragging along on the ground (make your line smaller and lighter as training progresses) and under no conditions can any dog tell where the end of a dragline is. So, a 20-foot (6.1-m) dragline makes you magically able to stop the dog if he decides to go in the wrong direction. The dog will never figure out how you do this. They don't understand radios, television, or electricity either. There are

some things that dogs just don't get and this is one of them that can be used greatly to our advantage.

In addition to control, another benefit of letting the lead stay on the floor is that it forces you to interact with the dog rather than continually using the lead to overwhelm him. The hand movements you develop in manipulating the dog into position with the food become the communication link that enables you to talk to the dog more eloquently as the training tasks become more complicated.

Chain-Breaker

I tried putting the *chain-breaker* further along in this chapter and discovered you really need this concept from the very beginning. So far as my research has indicated, no one else uses this particular command; there-

The Chain-Breaker Command: An Essential Communication Tool

Lack of understanding and proper use of this command is probably the single most likely reason fewer dogs attain the utility level than should. Many dogs, and owners, simply give up in frustration over inability to communicate when the messages get more complex. Do not skip this section; it is truly not an optional exercise.

fore, it needs to be addressed before you even start adding the more complex training steps that will eventually lead to the finished performance.

One of the basic problems that occurs in many obedience training programs involves the misunderstanding of the dog's perceived anticipation of the next exercise. For example, if the dog is told to do a *sit-stay*, the handler walks out, turns, and then calls the dog; the dog is expected to stay until the handler gives the *recall* command. When the dog fails to wait for the *recall* but comes as the handler turns, he is frequently forcefully corrected and returned to the *sit*. The dog experiences extreme frustration at this point because as far as he is concerned, he is doing the correct thing. As training progresses, there is a consistent chaining of the dog's correct response from one command to another. Some of the commands are oral, some hand signals, and some

body movements. Hooking the *turn* to the *recall* is simply another example of chaining as far as the dog is concerned and it is incomprehensible to the dog that there is a difference between this and similar learning experiences. The *turn* is the new command that owners need to focus on from the dog's point of view.

Continued corrections when the dog is doing what (he) thinks is right result in a dog that is confused, frustrated, and finally, depressed. Frequently the dog will develop a fear of failure that inhibits future learning. Continued corrections that the dog perceives as inconsistent and unfair will also cause gradual erosion of the dog's faith in the handler's judgment.

The best way to avoid this particular problem is to teach the dog a *"chain-breaking"* command. Using the *sit* and *recall* as an example, this is how you would proceed.

1. Sit the dog, walk away, turn, and execute the *recall*.

2. The first time the dog gets up as soon as you turn, go to the dog quietly and cross your hands in front of the dog several times.

3. Reposition the dog using hand signals and give the *stay* command.

4. As you walk away, turn back to face the dog every few feet making the hand-crossing motion.

5. Once in position, do the *recall*.

The first time you may have to run backward to get the dog going, but within a time or two, the dog will figure out what is going on and wait for the second command. As far as the dog goes, the *turn* will always represent the first command to come. However, dogs seem to experience little or no difficulty in accepting the concept of waiting for the second or even third, in some cases, command to act.

Incorrectly called anticipation, this is in reality a very common pattern called sequential learning. It is a normal continuation of the learning process you have been teaching your dog.

When to Use the Chain-Breaker

The major places you will use the *chain-breaker* command at the novice level are with the *recall* exercise, on the front before the finish, and between the *sit* and *down-stay*. If you go further into AKC obedience, there are over 30 places in which this exercise is absolutely essential.

Sometimes there are accidental cues that cause the dog to respond before the handler wants him to. These can be subtle or very obvious. Occasionally it is necessary to have someone videotape your performance and look very closely to determine what the dog is picking up on that you are missing. An excellent example is the slight dip of the head or shift of the shoulders just before giving the *recall*. Another is the handler looking at the judge to catch the signal for a *recall*. Some dogs will start to come as soon as your eyes shift to the judge and back to the dog. As you analyze what your dog is responding to during training, you may find it necessary to pass as many as three or four cues that seem reasonable to the dog in order to get to the one you want the dog to wait for.

What the *chain-breaker* tells the dog is to wait for the second, or in some cases the third, cue or command before proceeding. The *chain-breaker* is especially useful in teaching the *drop on recall* where it is used for places to tell the dog to wait for a command instead of reacting to sequence cues. Sitting when you stop when both you and the dog are facing the same direction is also a sequence cue. Another sequence cue the dog learns is that you always finish after a front in the ring. You may do 500 different things in practice, but the dog learns quickly what the sequence is in the ring—you cannot prevent this. It just shows the dog is paying attention. But with the use of the *chain-breaker*, you can train the dog to wait for the cue you want him to respond to.

At any point during training that the dog reacts before the critical cue, gently return him to the correct position, give the crossed-hands *chain-breaker* several times, then give the cue you want the dog to respond to. Praise and reward liberally. When you first introduce the crossed-hands signal, repeat it several times. Eventually once or twice will tell the dog this is a command he is to skip and wait for the next one. If you are giving two cues before the one you really want, put the *chain-breaker* before each until the dog zeroes in on the correct cue. While this may sound complicated, it is probably one of the best and easiest commands you can teach your dog. It increases communication and prevents your thinking in terms of correction instead of clarifying your intent.

Situational Cues: Besides sequential and accidental cues, you will also encounter situational cues. Situational cues are attached to a particular environment that is often apparent to the dog, but unnoticed by the handler. When the situation changes, the dog's response is affected. Understanding what is influencing the dog and helping the dog learn to respond correctly even when the environment is different is part of the advanced training referred to as proofing. Use as many positive cues and reinforcements to work through these problems as possible. Sometimes a *chain-breaker* command is useful and sometimes supportive, controlled, calm repetition of the desired behavior and response is best. These are often the most difficult problems to deal with and a positive approach will help your dog establish a higher degree of confidence in your judgment.

Remember, you can add a new command at any time simply by pairing it with one of the known commands. A new command word is frequently taught when you want to combine two or more basic commands into one. Examples include the *recall* (combining the *come* and *front*) and the *retrieve* over the jump (combining the *retrieve* with the *jump* and *come* commands). You can

chain routines in any desired manner, putting your breaks in wherever you need them. This all adds up to the type of communication that makes the use of force and corrections unnecessary distractions in your training program and produces a confident, happy, willing partner throughout both the training process and the eventual performance.

Do not lose sight of the fact that performance events are teamwork-oriented. If both members of the team are not confident in each other, the ultimate performance will suffer.

Stand for Novice and Utility

The *stand* is probably the easiest of all of the obedience exercises to teach. When you start the very young puppy or the older dog walking on the loose lead with the "*Let's go*" command, you eventually have to stop. Since you are not going to use the *sit* command until the dog can sit quickly and reliably on the word "*Sit*," you need another exercise to end the walking on loose lead. When you get ready to stop, take a step ahead of the dog on your right foot. This will bring you to a halt facing the dog's right shoulder. At the same time, lower your right hand with the food in it to a point directly in front of the dog's nose. The dog will stop because your hand with the food is in the way. The dog will stay standing because it is his nature to

This **stand** *is representative of the obedience* **stand** *for examination.*

do so. While he is eating the treat, say *"Good stand."* Reach over and give the two-pat release (two pats with your left hand on the dog's left side). Swing back into your normal walking position, say *"Let's go"* and be off again. Repeat this three times each session, and it won't be long until the dog will have a good foundation for the *stand* exercise. The dog will also have learned to stand as is required in the breed ring and for measuring in AKC obedience trials. Waiting to move until you give the two pats will lay the foundation for the *stays* to be taught later.

You might find the dog sits the first time you try this. It will generally be because you have held the food too high. The treat must be even with the dog's nose, and the nose must be level with the topline. In other words,

the dog must remain looking straight ahead, not up or down.

Sit for Front, Heeling, Long Sit, and Hand-Signal Sit

The nose-lift is the easiest of the *sit* techniques to teach, is retained longer by the dog than most other methods, has greater flexibility in its ability to be chained to other commands as the training progresses, and requires no training equipment. See Chapter Seven on puppies for details.

This is the first step in the chaining process for the exercise *"Sit."* After the dog has learned to sit on the nose-lift signal, the next step in the *sit* progression is adding the word "*Sit*." With the dog standing on a loose lead, put your hand with the treat in it (generally the right hand) behind your back before you give the command to sit. Do not bring the food out where the dog can see it until he is sitting or until you realize you will have to use the nose-lift to get the *sit*. Say "*Sit*," wait a second or two, and follow up with the nose-lift. Give the food and say "*Good sit*." Work in sets of three until he sits when you say "*Sit*." Continue to reward with "*Good sit*" and the food. The first week you will get some *sits* on the word, and some on the nose-lift. Continue practicing the sets of three until the dog can sit on the verbal command correctly on the first try three times in a row.

As soon as you get a reliable *sit* on the verbal command three times in a row for three different sessions, it is time to change the location of your practice area. Change the distance at which you give the command and the positions from which the dog must execute the command until the dog will sit on the verbal command regardless of the circumstances and up to at least a 40-foot (12-m) distance. No matter how good the dog gets, he will occasionally forget or make a mistake. Use the nose lift as a reminder.

It is imperative that the dog sits reliably on the verbal command before you try the *sit* with the walking-on-lead (or heeling) exercise or the *sit* at the end of the *Find it* exercise. Keep in mind that he is learning to chain responses together. Your dog is being rewarded for making these connections and should be exhibiting pleasure in his success. The dog may be a little slow to respond in the beginning. He must learn to think in a very different way and must also develop the ability to concentrate on an activity he did not initiate.

At this point in the *sit* training you will have to take a break until you and the dog have worked through the first part of the walking on lead section. When you can successfully keep the dog in the correct *heel* position, you will be ready to come back to this section and teach the dog the automatic *sit* in the *heel* position.

You can start working on *sit-stays* as soon as the dog has a good feeling for sitting on command. Sit the dog; give the verbal *Stay* and the hand signal. The hand signal is the open hand shown to the dog a few inches from his nose. Start with very short *stays*, just a few seconds. Release with two pats. To speed up the process, hook a 6-foot (1.8-m) lead to a doorknob and attach to the dog's collar. Let the dog come almost to the end of the lead, sit him, and give the *stay* command. This keeps the dog from coming toward you should he get up. If he does, simply use the nose lift *sit* to reposition him, repeat the *stay*, and try to get the *two-pat release* before the dog moves. Holding the dog with the food as you give the *release* makes this easier in the beginning.

Continue to increase the time between the *stay* command and the *two-pat release* until the dog will stay up to one or two minutes. Next start moving away from the dog a foot at a time until you can go up to 20 feet (6 m) and return without the dog moving. At this point, stop putting the dog on the door and start working the *stays* using only the leash on the floor if necessary for control.

Staying close, start leaving the dog on the *stay* from the *heel* position and returning to the dog and going all the way around him and back into *heel* position. Start with short time and distance and gradually build up his tolerance. As soon as the dog is staying until you return, increase the time away until you can walk out, stand for one to three minutes, and return to the dog in the *heel* position without the dog moving from his spot.

The *sit* from a *down* in the signal exercise can also be started as soon as the dog learns the *down*. The hand signal for the *sit* is a slightly exaggerated form of the nose-lift *sit*. Use the left hand, palm up, the gesture from right below the dog's head to just above it. Pair this with the nose-lift a few times and the dog should have no problems making the chain.

This exercise becomes more difficult as you increase the distance from the dog.

1. With the dog on a *down*, walk back a step or two and give the *sit* signal.

2. Return, reward, and release.

3. Keep moving back until you can sit the dog on the hand signal from 20 feet (6 m) away. This may take longer than some of the other exercises. Do not worry and do not rush it.

4. If the dog is not solid on the verbal *Sit*, this is harder to teach since you sometimes need to give the verbal when the dog doesn't sit on the hand command.

Another exercise you can also be working on is the *sit* at the end of the *Find-it*. Throw the food out a few feet and send the dog. As soon as the dog eats the food, tell him to sit. If he turns and sits, you will know you have done an excellent job of teaching the *sit* command. If he ignores the command and starts back, you can do one of two things. Either go back and work on the *sit* command

some more, or, when the dog gets to the food, be right behind him to reinforce the *sit* with the nose-lift. Work on this until the dog either comes back on the "*Here*" command or turns and sits on the *Sit* command.

After the *turn* and *sit*, either release the dog or go to another exercise such as the directed jump, which will be covered later under jumping.

Recall

One of the hardest concepts people have to understand in dealing with dogs is remembering that they are extremely precise in their idea of the meaning of words, much like three-year-old children. They cannot understand why "*Come*" means "*Come sit in front*" on some occasions, and just "*Get over here*" or "*Get in the house*" at other times. That is why you need the informal word "*Here*" for all *recalls* that are to get the dog in the house or simply close enough to pet or catch. "*Here*" is the foundation word upon which the more specific obedience command, "*Come*," is based. "*Come*" means to quit whatever he is doing and get into a straight *sit* in front of you as quickly as possible.

Front

The early "*Find it—Here*" sets the foundation for the *front*, watch me, and finish. Once the dog is coming back quickly to the "*Here*," use both hands holding the food directly in front of your body. To begin, you may lean toward the dog as he comes in, catching the nose with the food (getting the food close enough to the dog's nose so he smells it) and drawing the dog straight into you. Straighten up, still holding the food in both hands (this keeps the dog centered), and bring the dog's nose up to obtain a nose-lift *sit*. You will have to practice to get this exactly as you want it. Use a mirror placed so you can see how the dog is sitting in relation to you. The dog should be as close as possible without touching and sitting straight in front of you. Say "*Good Front*" or "*Good Come*," whichever you wish.

When you start, you can call "*Here, come, front*" and later drop the *Here*, and use either *Come* or *Front*. The command word is a matter of preference; just be consistent. Eventually, the dog will learn the total picture, including your position, the command, and the environment. Until the dog has accumulated many experiences, and sometimes even after, any change in one or more parts of the picture may alter the dog's performance. Those who intend to train for herding may want to select one of the alternate words to replace the traditional "*Come*" command as *Come* and *Come Bye* are used in an entirely different context in that activity.

Watch

As soon as your dog comes in and assumes the correct position when you are standing straight and not leaning toward him, you are ready to begin the *watch* exercises.

The first one is done with the dog directly in front of you.

1. Hold both hands by your side with a piece of bait in each. The first time you move your hands to your side, the dog will look at your hands.

2. Catch his attention with your voice (whisper, make small noises, whistle) but be careful not to distract him enough to move away.

3. Lure the dog into looking up at your face. As soon as the dog glances up into your face, and preferably makes eye contact, reward and praise with "*Good watch*."

The reward should come straight down from your nose to the dog. Some handlers spit the food from their mouth to the dog. This requires two things: the dog must be able to catch the food and the handler must be able to hold food without eating it. Since I have problems with both of these, my solution is to quickly bring the food up to a point just above my nose, then take it straight down to the dog's mouth. You can use either hand and should alternate to keep the dog from expecting the food from one hand or the other. Eventually it doesn't matter where the food is for the dog learns that only by maintaining eye contact does he get the reward. In the beginning use the command "*Watch me*." This is the major step in removing the food from the front exercise.

Do only one or two of these the first day. Gradually include one or two in each set of *fronts* until the dog learns he must look at you and not look away in order to get the treat. As the dog develops concentration, praise should be sufficient to maintain the dog's interest. However, should a distraction problem develop, go back to the food until it is resolved.

Eventually the dog should come in, sit, and maintain eye contact until released or given another command.

Later the *finish* will be included. If, at that point, the dog attempts to go to heel before being given the command, use the *chain-breaker* command and continue working.

Note that all of this training is done off lead (let the lead drag or use a dragline if you need it for control or safety). Since there is only one exercise performed on lead in novice and that is the on-lead heeling, there is very little reason to teach the dog to do much lead work beyond normal walking on lead to go places where the rules or safety require him to be on leash.

The problem with the leash is that it can quickly become a necessary part of the environment for the dog if it is continually in the dog's line of sight. Use your body and the food to keep the dog in the correct position. The habits you both develop early will keep you going together later.

Eventually, you will be doing a *recall* from a *sit* at about 40 feet (12 m). *Recalls* from a *sit* should be done sparingly. Remember to use the *chain-breaker* to avoid having the dog come before called.

Down for Drop on Recall, Long Down, Hand-Signal Down

The *down* exercise is taught in three steps and can be started with any age dog from six weeks up. The same method is used with older dogs and is especially useful in correcting problems that might have developed through ineffective training. Review step one, the nose-drop *down* in Chapter Seven.

Do not give the *down* command at this point in the training. Just continue to go through the motions until you get a successful *down* and then praise.

After the dog has learned additional cues, the *down* will be done from the *stand*, the basic position while standing still, moving both from a walk and a run, and finally at

a distance of 50 or more paces at the end of a go-out. The *down* will also be used in several Schutzhund exercises as well as in both herding and tracking. In tracking, the optimum way to indicate when an article is found is to have the dog lie down beside it. Having been taught the nose drop makes the article indication in tracking an extremely easy and natural exercise for the dog.

Do three of these exercises at each practice session for at least one week. As soon as the dog is going down quickly when you point to the ground, then move to the next level. Hold the food behind you and raise your left leg until the knee is bent. Do this where the dog can readily see your knee. Lower your foot to the ground and do the nose-drop *down*, reward and say "*Good down*." Do this until the dog is going down when you cock your knee. You

should make the knee lift in an exaggerated manner in the beginning, but gradually reduce this until you lift your foot up only about one foot off the ground. We have chained the pointing to the ground command to a knee-lift command, so you now have another cue for the *down*. This exercise is rarely used in competition but is an excellent bridge in training many of the *down* exercises. Bridges are communication doors that make it easier for a dog to get from one step to another.

When the dog can do both the nose-drop and knee-lift *down* smoothly and quickly, with the food out of sight, say "*Down*" and give the knee lift immediately. Always praise with "*Good down*" so the dog continually hears the word "*Down*" when in the *down* position.

Variable Reinforcement

Use the food treats until the dog is working reliably, then alternate the use of food with the word "*Good*." Do this in a random manner so the dog never knows when it will or will not get a food treat along with the reinforcer "*Good*." This is called variable reinforcement. Continual reinforcement (give a treat each time the dog does it right) is the best way to establish the learning in the beginning but variable reinforcement has been proven to be the most reliable way to set training once it has been accomplished. If, at any time during the training, or later during practice, the dog fails to respond to the word "*Down*," use whichever of the above visual cues that you need to get the correct response. The dog will forget the spoken word much more quickly than any of the physical cues and will also become more easily confused when you start adding other words to his vocabulary. It will probably be necessary at some time or another to remind the dog with the physical cues (nose-drop or knee-lift commands), regardless of how long you practice and/or perform.

When you switch to the verbal command, make certain the dog doesn't pick up hand signals with the food. Put the hand with the treat behind you or out of sight of the dog. After the dog exhibits a reliable response, you can put the food on a table or chair and give it only after the dog has completed the exercise.

As soon as the dog has mastered the knee-lift *down*, you can use that reminder to keep him down until you give the two-pat release. Now you will be building the *stay* with more regularity, as you have more tools to work with in communicating to the dog exactly what you expect of him.

You will need to practice having the dog go down from a walk, run, on the end of the lead, and finally running away from you. This is another place where the "*Find it—Here*" exercise is invaluable. Throw the food out for the dog, "*Find it*," and have the dog *down* before returning. Since you can control the direction and distance of the food, you can set the dog up to go down as he is going after the food, after he has eaten the food, or as he is returning to you.

Group Exercises

You will need to get other handlers and have them line their dogs up about 2 feet (6 cm) apart so your dog can get practice doing the group *long sit* and *long down* as required by the AKC. After the dog has some maturity and experience, you can start going out of sight for a short period of time when doing this exercise. Build up your time until the dog can tolerate your being out of sight for five minutes. The AKC requires a *long sit* of one minute and a *long down* of three minutes. While in novice the handlers stand in sight and are only about 30 feet (9 m) away. At the open level, the dogs are required to *sit* for three minutes and *down* for five minutes while the handlers are out of sight.

One of the AKC exercises requires the dog to be called about 40 feet (12 m) from a *sit* and dropped to a *down* about halfway in, then recalled to a *front* from the *down* position. This is called the "*drop on recall*" and is used in the open class (second level) of AKC competition. The use of the "*Find it—Here*" makes training the *down* when the dog is in motion and at a distance much easier on both the handler and the dog.

Always remember to use one of the physical cues, such as the knee lift, the nose-drop, or the hand signal, for "*Down*" if the dog forgets the word. Time and lots of repeats make this exercise reliable and fast. Use the *chain-breaker* to prevent the dog from coming before called, dropping before the command, and from coming in before the *recall from the down* is given.

If, at any time during the training or polishing, the dog gets up (breaks the *sit* or *down* by moving out of position), do not punish him. Use the *chain-breaker* command, take the dog back, *sit* or *down* him, then work a little closer for a few sets. Gradually build up the dog's tolerance for distance, time, and having you out of sight. The more gradually you work these exercises, the more reliable they will be in the future.

Finish

The judge will say or give you a signal to "*finish*." Except for the *finish* to *heel* in utility, the dog will be sitting in front of you, either from a *recall*, *retrieve*, or *return* over a jump. On command, the dog is expected to move sharply from in front of you into the correct *heel* position.

There are two ways for the dog to get back into *heel* position. One is to swing to his right, pivoting his rear around until he is sitting on your left in *heel* position. The other is to pass to your right, behind you, and down your left side stopping in a *sit* in the correct position. Many people like the *pass* with large dogs; however, I don't want my dog out of sight (behind me) as it opens up too many avenues for distractions. The *swing* is no harder for a German Shepherd Dog to accomplish than the *pass*. Both are taught off lead with food. Some trainers use the *heel* command for the *finish*. It works; however, it would seem that clearer communication would result in using separate commands leaving *Heel* to mean only one thing: we are going to go forward briskly until another cue is given. *Finishes* always end up in the dog sitting, while *Heel* always means the dog is going to move out. It may be a fine point, but that is often what makes the difference in the final performance.

Since you use the food to get the dog into *heel* position rather than the collar/lead, you will find that you have developed the knack of swinging the dog into the basic *heel* position with the food in order to start most exercises. Now you are going

Once you give the command Stand, *the dog should remain in that position until released, even if the handler walks away.*

to formalize this act to move the dog from a *front* position into the *heel*, or basic position, using the food.

Swing

For the *swing*, with the dog sitting in front, bring the treat in your left hand up to the dog's nose. Give the command "*Swing*." This lets the dog know something new is going to happen. As he reaches for the food, move it to your left in a fairly wide arc, causing the dog to start to pass you on your left. At the same time take two steps straight back. Bring the dog's nose in toward you, then take two or more steps forward to bring the dog into *heel* position. Do a nose-lift *sit*, praise, and reward. It may take one or two tries to get the rhythm for you and your dog. Do a few each day.

Eventually, you will reduce your steps to one and finally you will stay put and take the dog around using

only your arm movement and food. Watch to see if he moves on the command or is waiting for the food to move. The final goal will be for the dog to go on the command or the hand signal. As the dog becomes more skilled in picking up the cue, the hand signal will become shorter until only a gesture to the left is needed to get the dog into the correct position.

Use the *chain-breaker* to hold the dog in the *front* position until you give the signal to move to *heel* while you are training and you will rarely have a dog that goes to *heel* before the command.

As with all exercises, food is gradually phased out through intermittent rewards over a period of time. When working on performance exercises, there should always be occasional food rewards offered at random times and for random sections. There should always remain in the dog's mind the hope of possible extra reward. Praise is forever the German Shepherd Dog's major pleasure in life, but food runs a very close second.

Heel and Footwork, Right-Foot Lead, and Hand Signal

While practicing *"Let's go,"* start working on getting the dog into the correct *heel* position. Use the food in your left hand to guide the dog into the correct position. *Heel* position, whether the dog is sitting, standing, lying down, or moving at *heel* is the same. The dog must be in a straight line with the direction in which the handler is facing, at the handler's left side, and as close as practical to the handler's left leg without crowding. The area from the dog's head to shoulder should be in line with the handler's left hip. The head starts with the dog's nose and the shoulder ends with the back of the shoulder blade. If you dropped a line from your waist to the floor centered on your hip, it should fall within that area.

Use a mirror to see if you have the dog in the correct position. When he is, say *"Good heel"* and reward. As you work, keep trying to get the dog into the correct position and quickly return your left hand to the belt buckle position. Work your hand from there back to reward the dog. Eventually the dog will learn that you are going to bring the food back to him if he stays in that position. *"Heel"* is a moving positional command.

Do not add the *sit* until you can keep the dog moving briskly in the correct *heel* position for at least 20 or 30 paces. Also, the dog must have a good verbal *sit* command. As you are heeling along, tell the dog to sit. If the dog fails to sit, use the nose-lift *sit* command to remind him. If the dog is out of position, take a few steps forward to line the dog up correctly and repeat the *sit* and halt. If you do not get a good *heel-sit*, try it again using the bait to maneuver the dog into the correct *sit* position with a nose-lift *sit*. You may have to do a couple of these before you get the feel of where the dog's nose needs to be in order for the rear to be in the correct position when the *sit* is completed. If you hold the food too far to the dog's right, his rear end will swing out away from you. If you hold the food too far to the dog's left, the dog's rear will swing behind you. Either of these positions will result in a crooked *sit*. Also, holding the food too far in front of the dog will result in a forged (dog in front of correct heel position) *sit*. A little practice should make you expert in putting the dog exactly where you want him to be. This is especially helpful in polishing the dog's final *sits* so they are exactly where they should be. Line yourself and the dog up in front of a full-length mirror when practicing this exercise so you can see your position when you stop. If your dog wants to swing his rear out away from you, heel close to a barrier (wall, couch, etc.) and stop so that when the dog sits he has to sit straight.

Do only a few of these at a time until you can keep the dog in the correct position and execute the above exercise correctly.

As you and your dog become more skillful in maintaining position and stopping correctly, start incorporating right, left, and about turns. Eventually add the slow and fast sections. Introduce each new element individually over a period of time.

This is an intensely difficult exercise and requires the utmost in concentration from both the handler and the dog. Short work sessions mixed up with other exercises that are less stressful will enhance both the learning and performance. More dogs are

Teaching the puppy to sit when looking up makes getting front sits *easy.*

ruined by overtraining on heeling than any other exercise. If you can gradually work up to one minute of correct heeling you will have little difficulty in competition.

Once you have the dog sitting correctly with the nose-lift, the next step will be to take several steps, then give the dog the command to "*Sit*" as you stop on your right foot. Bring your left foot up and halt. Make sure the dog's feet are straight and even.

When the dog sits at your stopping without any additional cue, you will have the automatic *sit*. The dog will have chained your body movements (the way you come to a halt and the direction you are facing) connected with stopping to the *sit* command. Since this is the response you want, this is a good chain.

Halt and Forward

You can add verbal cues by having someone call "*Halt*" and *Forward* so the dog gets used to hearing the judge's commands. If the dog starts to respond on the judge's cues, give the *chain-breaker* and work until the dog understands that the judge's cue means to get ready but wait for your command before responding. If you do not have a partner to work with, put the commands on a tape recorder with space between for heeling. You will find that the dog will begin heeling on your hand signal without the verbal cue very easily. In performance for novice and open you can use either voice or hand signal for heeling, but in utility you must use signals only.

Do only a few heeling exercises at a time, working until you can keep the dog in the correct position and execute the above exercise correctly.

Once the dog is staying in *heel* position and doing automatic *sits*, it is time to start concentrating on your footwork. Practice all footwork separately first. Add the dog only after you feel confident and relaxed with your body movements.

The Origins of Dog Obedience

In the beginning, dog obedience was a function of service dog training in Europe. Service dog training was done primarily by men who had previous military service. As you are all aware, in the military, it is the custom to start all marching on the left foot. What is probably lost in antiquity, but was more than likely thought up by some enterprising ancient soldier in order to enforce military uniformity and make the teaching of marching easier. Anyway, when the early dog trainers started heeling, they unconsciously started off on the left foot as a holdover from their military training. No one challenged this practice, so it became the custom.

When obedience training moved to America, it was started by two men steeped in the European obedience-service dog traditions. They started on the left foot, so everyone else did. Then, as time passed, someone asked why. Instructors started looking for a justification of the left-foot start. At first glance it seems logical that the dog can see the left foot move and move with it, so that was the offered reason. It works for the average dog, and the exceptional dog can overcome most adverse conditions to rise above them, so no one challenged this method in the beginning. My first question when given this explanation was: If the dog is expected to see a hand signal at 40 feet (12 m), why can't he see the right leg when it moves less than one foot away? Many people have told me that they start on their left leg and leave the dog sitting on their right leg. Sounds good until you analyze it. Just for kicks, squat down beside a friend in the *heel* position. Look up at your friend. Have her give you a "*Stay*" command, then use the hand signal *stay* and step away. If you are looking up, as your dog should be, and she places her hand in front of your eyes, there is no way you can tell which foot she started out on. Plus, think about this—you have given two verbal commands (*sit* and *stay*) and a hand signal, if your dog doesn't stay on those, he probably won't pay a great deal of attention to your footwork.

Today there are many research projects going on and there is information coming in from all over the world that enlightens us to the ways dogs think and learn. The results of these studies are giving creative instructors food for thought and are leading them to think, as nearly as possible, from the dog's point of view. This results in more attempts to modify the training methods to fit the dog's frame of reference instead of the handler's. So, back to the right foot versus the left foot from the dog's point of view.

If you start on your left foot, you will often be 6 to 8 to 10 inches (15 to 20 to 25 cm) ahead of your dog before he realizes you are moving. As the dog starts to get up, he will have to speed up to catch up. This often causes him to overshoot the *heel* position and have to adjust his pace. If the dog is well trained, he will eventually fall into the correct *heel* position. Some breeds are extra quick and a few individuals within almost any breed can be found that can do an "instant" start, but the

While obedience instruction is extremely important, the socialization process, where dogs get used to both people and other dogs, is of equal value.

majority of German Shepherd Dogs will do the *lag, forge, adjust* routine nearly every time they start up. This will cause a major point loss in obedience competition.

If, however, you start on your right foot things are different. The dog can see that you are moving away, so he will elevate his rear end at about the same time your right foot touches the ground. Your left leg, which hasn't moved yet, is still in the *heel* position with the dog. As you move your left leg forward, the dog is already standing and ready to move forward with you smoothly and in place. This happens very quickly in "real time" but it makes all the difference in today's obedience ring where points are critical. If you videotape this or work on it while looking in a mirror, you will see that you cannot extend your right leg without your entire upper body moving forward. This is a major body cue telling the dog that you are going. Compare this with moving your left foot first. You will see very little upper body movement until the right leg starts to move. In other words, you can take a major step forward with your left foot and keep your body straight; you cannot do this with the right foot.

Performance as Kinetic Learning

Performance is a kinetic learning experience. This is true both for you and the dog. Motor movements are memorized until they become automatic. Responses to motor movements also become automatic over time. Knowing this should help you analyze potential problems and figure out ways to fix them instead of trying to put the blame on the dog being difficult or stupid. Probably very few really good performers are exceptionally brilliant; they are more likely to be a team that has learned how to cope with their problems and enhance their skills. A good rule of thumb is never blame the dog for any failure. Never consider any failure more than another opportunity to learn something about you and/or your dog. And when you stop enjoying the dog and having fun working, stop. If this happens frequently, you might want to reevaluate your choice of sports.

As training progresses, the dog will come to realize that the right leg signals movement and the left leg signals direction. Thus, you are

establishing communication at the level of the dog's comprehension that is highly keyed to body movements.

We have found through research that this simple change in body movement from starting on the left foot to starting on the right will often raise the scores for some dogs as much as five to ten points in the heeling exercises. It takes little effort, and can produce wonderful results in the show ring.

Since we are using the right foot to initiate movement in the heeling segment of the exercises, it is easy to use the left foot to designate direction. If you slightly point your left toe to the left, then step around on your right foot, your dog will make a smooth left turn. On right turns, place your left foot slightly in front of your right foot while pointing your left foot to the right. Step around the turn on your right foot and your dog will have time to make a smooth right-hand turn. Practice these two exercises without the dog first. Add the dog only after you feel comfortable with the movements. You will notice that you take slightly shorter steps to make these turns smoother. However, you do not want the final performance to reflect any reduction in your normal walking speed. Never use the word "*Heel*" to replace "*Let's go*." "*Heel*" is competition-specific. "*Let's go*" is general and is used most of the time. Dogs will even learn to sit when you stop in the "*Let's go*" exercise, providing you are both facing in the same direction. "Let's go" is very easy and

relaxed and is the basic loose-lead exercise used for the majority of the dog's regular activities.

Superb Heeling in Competition

If you want superb heeling in competition, keep the sessions short and remember you must never do this exercise in the beginning with a leash in your hand as the dog will relate to the presence of the leash and behave differently when the leash is later removed. Leashes are used only for conformation and going for a walk. The one exception to this is the *heel on lead* in novice obedience. That is a very short exercise and most dogs do not even notice that the lead is there. The one possible disadvantage of this method is that the dog may revert to the "*Let's go*" and be slightly more informal than you would like. But, remember, that is only one exercise and it's at the bottom level. All competition in open and utility is done off lead. The benefits of off-lead training become increasingly apparent as you progress through the more difficult levels.

This has worked very well with many breeds that have finished champion and obedience titles over the years. They do not appear to get these two exercises confused when they are taught with food and no force. We never jerk a dog into *heel* position as this tends to create a negative feeling in the German Shepherd Dog, which often gives the dog a depressed look when performing. Jerking also seems to set up a counter response that induces lagging and swinging wide in many dogs.

When you start practicing turns as you are heeling, you need to reinforce in your own mind how the dog operates. The dog is going to cue in on the movement of your left leg. That is the directional guiding leg for the dog. You will give an advanced signal to turn by pointing your left foot in the direction you intend to turn. You will do this on the last step before making the turn. When you are ready to turn to the left, make a step that keeps you facing straight ahead but points your left foot slightly to the left. This should be done with the left foot slightly in front of your right foot. Next, make a small step and bring your right foot around just slightly past your left foot. Step out on the left foot in a normal walk, having completed a left turn.

When you get ready to turn to the right, you will place the left foot slightly in front of the right and pointed right in the direction of the turn. Bring the right foot slightly past the left and then resume your normal walking gait, having completed a right turn.

Note: Whenever you desire a change in direction, always use the left foot to indicate to the dog the direction of change. The dog will not see it in the foot, but will get the message through your entire body torque. This is especially vital when you are doing any type of weaving in-and-out exercises. The AKC figure-eight turn, which is maneuvered around and between two people standing still, is a good example of this. A number of people walk naturally with their toes pointing outward. If they walk this way while doing the figure-eight, the dog will swing wide on all outside turns as he tries to follow the body torque that results from the outward-pointing left foot. Jerking the dog simply adds to his confusion. After all, the dog was trying to do what he thought he had been taught to do—follow the movements of the handler's left side. Often handlers must practice walking with their toes pointing in the correct direction of travel if they wish to do this exercise smoothly and not confuse their dogs.

Figure Eight

Start with a large figure-eight pattern. This allows you to move briskly and set up the flow of right and left curves. Gradually make the pattern tighter until you can work around two posts (people or objects) about 8 feet (2.4 m) apart. Encourage the dog to move faster on the straight line between the turns going into the right circle. Ease the dog into a slightly slower gait moving into the left circle. Eventually you will maintain the same pace while the dog will speed up on the outside and slow down on the inside. Don't do too many *halts* during practice, as this tends to slow the dog down.

About-Turn

The *about-turn* is like a dance step. When done smoothly it allows the dog to float around the turn with no interference from you and no confusion. In the beginning it takes a little more time and concentration on your part; however, eventually you will be able to do it without thinking. Bear in mind that you are asking the dog to learn multiple difficult exercises; you should be willing to learn a little to help him out.

As you approach the *about-turn*, place your right foot down, move your left foot so it is pointing to your right, and your instep is centered on the toe of your right foot. Turn your body to the right, place your right heel close to your left heel but slightly forward and facing forward. Bring your left foot around and place it slightly ahead of your left foot facing forward. Step off on your right foot and resume walking.

If you have difficulty keeping your left foot pointing right with the instep centered on your right toe, ease your left foot back until your left toe is even with your right toe. If this is still too stressful for your left leg muscles, just go as far as is comfortable, then continue.

This is a very smooth *about-turn* that doesn't interfere with the dog, gives the dog time to get around you, and presents a uniformly smooth picture. Don't slow down; however, you will find when you do this, it takes you a little longer to make the turn than a simple spin or abrupt change in direction. That is the key to helping your dog. It slows you down enough for him to make the turn without appearing that you slowed down, a move that could result in a point loss.

This exercise is well illustrated on tape in one of the OPT advanced obedience videos. The videos are a great assist when used in conjunction with this book.

While working on *heel* position, the dog must also be trained to watch the handler on command and remain watching until given the release or another command. As you work this exercise, try to keep in large circles (20 to 30 feet [6.1 to 9 m] across). Reverse the direction of the circle to include a large figure-eight. Remember to point your toes in the direction you intend to travel.

As the dog gets more efficient in staying in the *heel* position and looking at you, bring your left hand quickly to the belt-buckle position. Do not hold it there very long at first. Immediately return your hand to the dog's nose and give the reward. The goal is to gradually increase the length of time you can hold your hand in the buckle position and have the dog stay looking at you and correctly heeling until you bring the food back to him. The dog does not have to be looking at your face. Looking at your hand will achieve the same results and is much easier on the dog's neck.

Use very short work sessions but as many of them as you can work into your daily schedule. This lets the dog know that if he concentrates and finishes, he can then go play or do whatever he enjoys. Several one-minute sessions of heeling and on-lead exercises are better than one session that extends for ten minutes or more. Thirty seconds of heeling is sufficient in the beginning. Make everything short, smooth, business-like, and, if possible, enjoyable.

It is a good idea to avoid making this entire experience one giant game for the dog. Imagine what happens on a day when the dog doesn't feel like playing? All you have to do is drive 12 hours, rent a motel, pay an entry fee, and then stand out in the field and try to get your dog going on a day when he doesn't feel like playing your game. After a few experiences on that order, you will soon lose faith in the "it's all fun and games" theory of dog training. Think about Seeing Eye dogs. They enjoy their work but realize that it is neither a game nor an optional exercise.

Show the dog what must be done, make it easy, understandable, and through consistency of routine, inevitable.

Remember, in all training the three basic steps are positively getting first response, establishing kinetic responses paired to positive reinforcers, and proofing to reliability. An old teaching adage, "learn in private, practice in public," works equally well for dogs.

Hand Positions

As you work on the heeling exercise, keep thinking about the positions that are allowed for your hands. This is important when using the food so the dog comes to associate certain hand positions with the possibility of rewards. There are no specific restrictions on hand placement in the *heel on lead* exercise. I prefer to hold my left hand on the belt-buckle position and let the right one swing. The leash should be held in the hands so as not to interfere with either you or the dog and should be loose enough to form a slight "J" before the hook meets the collar. Many people hold both hands on the belt-buckle position, and, while this is not incorrect, it involves separate training since you cannot put your right hand in that position for any exercise after the novice *heel on lead*.

In off-lead heeling, you have only two options for arm placement. You can go with the left hand on the belt buckle and right hand swinging or both arms swinging. Any other hand positions will be penalized. Personally, I feel that swinging the left arm is often a distraction to a dog you would like to pay attention to what your hands are saying. If you are short, you will have to do something with your swinging left arm to keep from hitting the dog in the back of the head. Swinging both arms is later used to cue the dog that you are doing a "*fuss*" or German type of heeling for the Schutzhund (Sch) competition. Since that is the only option for Sch, how short people can deal with this will be addressed in the Schutzhund section.

I train mainly with a nylon plastic snap collar or occasionally a cotton choke and a 4-foot (122-m) soft nylon lead. When showing sometimes I use a decorative chain slip, but more often I use a cotton slip collar fitted with just enough slack to comfortably slip over the dog's head. I also like a short, rather thin lead that is easy to tuck up into the hand out of sight. Whatever you plan to use in the ring should be introduced occasionally during training. Final polishing sessions should be as near ring conditions as possible to help familiarize the dog with as many distractions as possible.

Lineup

While working on the heeling and watch exercises, you can start teaching the left turn in place to line up the dog for the formal heeling exercises.

The best place to start any performance is at the beginning, but sometimes that is more difficult than it looks. When you enter the ring, the dog is on lead in novice and off lead for open and utility. Regardless, you still have to move from the ring gate to the point at which the first obedience exercise will begin. There are two ways to get into position. One is to *heel* or give the "*Let's go*" command up to the spot and do a *halt*. However, many times this is not easy since the start is close to the end of the mat. The worst way to line up is with an *about-turn* and *halt*. This causes the dog to overshoot and sit crooked most of the time. It also has a tendency to slow the dog down on *about-turns* in the heeling exercises when you want a performance that is both quick and brisk.

The easiest way to bring a dog into a straight sitting position for the start of any obedience exercise is to do a left turn in place, ending up facing the desired direction. Approach from the south, give the command "*Place*" or "*Line up*." Any suitable command will do; just be consistent. Use the food to keep the dog in position and do an *about-turn* to your left while keeping the dog on your left. As you get close to the desired position (both of you facing north), give the "*Sit*" command. As you practice this, make your turns tighter and neater until they are practically in one place. Keep your feet close together and remember to point your toes in your direction of travel.

Ideally you will give the command, point your left foot to the left, take a short close step across with your right foot, then point your left foot in the direction you will finish in and bring your right foot alongside. It may take a good deal of practice to get this exercise smooth and tight. Even a little loose, this procedure is still far more efficient on the *lineup* than the *about-turn*.

Once a dog learns this maneuver, he will always assume a sitting position when you do it. This keeps the dog from becoming confused on *about-turns* where you want the dog to go briskly and without hesitation. The left turn in place can be used any time you want the dog to line up for an exercise and end in a *sit*. Later, this may also be used in utility as one of the turns for the directed retrieve. In Rally, the left *about-turn* can be signaled with a different verbal command to avoid confusion.

Formal Retrieve

All puppies should be taught the foundation exercises at six to eight weeks as part of their early puppy training. Many puppies do not retrieve in play and many adult dogs were simply not exposed to this form of training as puppies and therefore do not understand the basic principle of bringing things back to their owners. There are many natural retrievers, and retrieving is a fun thing to do. My personal experience (and most research tends to support these observations) is that a dog will do better, regardless of how good a natural retriever he may be, if taught systematically what *"Take it," "Hold," "Carry,"* and *"Fetch"*

mean. If problems develop later, you will have established a basic communication system to help correct them. This systematic training is also extremely useful when teaching the dog to carry new and different objects. It is also a great foundation for advanced obedience training as detailed in the OPT videos.

Force

There are many available methods for teaching a dog to retrieve. Force is the least rewarding and most inefficient in the long run. The OPT is an extract of some of the most useable ideas combined with a few tricks I learned when I taught my horse to retrieve years ago for a rodeo act. Mixed with excerpts from research from around the world, the OPT method makes for a very reliable and easy-to-accomplish *retrieve*.

Treats

The method presupposes that the dog will eat treats. If he doesn't, you can do the *repeats* using only the word *"Good,"* but the results will be much slower. Sometimes dogs that refuse to eat treats require special methods, but fortunately they are an extremely small minority.

Repeats

It takes several hundred *repeats* for a dog to really learn. With this method, *repeats* can be accomplished in a relatively short time. All dogs do not learn at the same rate, nor do they all have the same attention span. Some will take several months to grasp parts of the retrieving exercise, while others may be able to complete the entire program in two days. But, both the fast and the slow learners will develop into equally cheerful and reliable workers in the end. I had a German Shepherd Dog bitch that did the entire program in two days. I had an Australian Cattle Dog bitch that took several months.

How to Start *Retrieve* Training

When you start *retrieve* training, you can use a straw, a pencil, a wood dowel cut to an appropriate length, the end of an old broom handle, or a regular dumbbell. Size will be determined by the dog's mouth capacity at the time. Straws are super for small puppies and even some larger dogs that show active resistance at the beginning of the training. If the dog has had a previous bad experience and you are using the OPT to correct a problem, it is generally best to start with a straw.

1. Find a quiet place to work. You don't need much room, but the area should be free of interruptions and distractions. The rule is to train in an area with no distractions so the dog can concentrate on learning new material. Once the training is thoroughly learned, it can be set or proofed by practicing under as many distractions as possible.

2. Set out your bait in three rows of three bits (that's nine pieces in all). You can work this anywhere with or without the dog having the collar and lead on. If the dog has a tendency to

wander away during training, put the collar and lead on and let it drag so you can step on the lead if he starts to wander. It makes no difference whether the dog sits or stands.

3. Take the dumbbell (or whatever you are using) and show it to the dog along with one piece of food. Try to get the dog to reach for the food, then put the dumbbell between the dog's nose and the food. Some dogs will immediately open their mouth at the sight of the food.

4. Put the dumbbell in his mouth as you say "*Take it*," and immediately say "*Give*," removing the dumbbell while giving the food. If, after a few tries, you cannot induce the dog to open his mouth, reach under the dog's lower jaw and gently open the mouth. Insert the dumbbell as you say "*Take it*" and immediately remove it as you say "*Give*."

5. Reward and repeat until you have used the first three goodies. I sometimes straddle the dog and work over his head on the first few *repeats*. This seems to give the dog support and reassurance. It is also easier to open the mouth from the lower jaw in this position.

6. Avoid putting your hand over the top of the dog's mouth to open it in teaching the *retrieve*. This is an exceptionally dominant gesture associated by most dogs with early corrections from adult dogs and can cause serious resentment, confusion, and other difficulties in learning this exercise.

Remember, we are going to train the dog in stages. The final goal will be "*Fetch*," which translates to the dog as "*Go out, pick up an item, bring it straight to me, sit in front, and hold it until I give you the command to let it go.*" That is a lot of response to expect from a one-word command, so teach it in several steps, giving a command word to each step. Later you will chain all of these together to get the finished product. Having these different steps in the chain will facilitate problem solving in the future.

After each set of three *repeats* and rewards, walk the dog around for 10 to 15 seconds—a short circle will do nicely—and then do the next three. Repeat this until you have rewarded the dog with all nine bits of food. Allow the dog to rest for at least 10 to 15 minutes at this point before doing another set or going on to another exercise. It is best to put the dog in his crate during this rest period if possible. This seems to facilitate the learning process.

Timing is important in this training, but you will have the opportunity to learn it as you go. As soon as the dog will take the dumbbell when it is presented, check to see if you are giving the command to "*Take it*" just before the dog does. Then make sure you say "*Give*" before you try to remove the dumbbell from the dog's mouth. Continue to pair the word "*Good*" with the food so that you will eventually have a super secondary reinforcer in the word "*Good*," and then you will not always need the food to reinforce the dog.

As the dog learns, you should also improve your handling and coordination with the dumbbell and the food.

1. Try holding the bit of food between your little finger and hand while gripping the dumbbell with the rest of your fingers as you make the presentation with your right hand.

2. As soon as the dog releases the dumbbell, you can rotate your hand and let the dog have the food from the same hand that just took the dumbbell. (For left-handed people, put the food between the little finger and hand of the left hand and present the dumbbell with the left hand. If you are reaching over the dog to open his mouth, use your right hand from under the jaw.)

3. Walking the dog in a short circle after each of the three *repeats* will relax the dog and you. This is especially true if the dog is a bit tense and offers some resistance at first.

4. If you are working with a very young puppy, do only three *repeats* at each session—you will not need the intervening walks. With mature dogs, you can continue work sessions with a ten-minute crate rest or a break for the functions of nature, so long as you do not overfeed the dog or until you, the dog, or both, get tired. Also remember to offer the dog a drink of water at regular intervals.

5. If all goes well, the dog should be taking the dumbbell on command after the first three or four sessions without your having to open his mouth. Most dogs will be opening their mouth to receive the dumbbell within ten sets (90 *repeats*). Some dogs take longer, some do it much faster, but that is about the average time.

6. As soon as the dog opens his mouth on the command "*Take it*," try making him reach a short distance for the dumbbell—very short at first. Use the food just beyond the dumbbell as motivation for this part. Talk to your dog enthusiastically, move away, and try to get him to follow. This is a form of teasing that should lure the dog into participating in the training process. When the dog will reach and take the dumbbell on the command nine times in a row, you are ready to teach the "*Hold*."

7. When the dog takes the dumbbell, use your hand in an attention-getting gesture—palm to the dog's nose without touching and a slight in-and-out movement. Say "*Hold*." Wait three to five seconds, then say "*Give*."

8. Take the dumbbell and reward him. Hold the dumbbell with one hand and give the signal with the other hand. Do not turn the dumbbell loose at this point, even though the dog appears to be holding it.

As soon as you can get the dog to hold the dumbbell for ten seconds with your holding it lightly, try getting a hold for three seconds without touching it. Gradually build up to ten seconds. When the dog can do this nine times in a row, you are ready to move to the next step.

The next step is a little tricky, so give yourself and the dog plenty of time.

1. Hold the dumbbell out in front of the dog, use the lead lightly and gently if necessary, and get the dog to walk toward the dumbbell on the command "*Take it*." At first the dog will walk to the dumbbell, then freeze once he gets the dumbbell in his mouth.

2. Let the dog hold the dumbbell a few seconds, then take it out.

3. All the time, remember to praise and reward and continue the routine where you do three, walk around, do three, walk around, do three, and stop for at least ten minutes. This is called a set.

The goal at this stage is to get the dog walking, have him take the dumbbell, and then take a few steps with the dumbbell without dropping it. If the dog does drop it, simply pick it up, show the dog the food, explain that he gets no reward for dropping the dumbbell, and proceed with the training. Getting the dog through this stage may take a while, so don't get impatient and try to short-cut with force. Eventually, with enthusiasm (be lavish with your praise at this point and use lots of encouragement), the dog will catch on. The dog is not only learning to retrieve, but also learning to learn. That is the most important concept that any student (whether human or animal) can ever master in the learning process.

Keep working on the dog taking the dumbbell from your hand while moving and then continuing to move while holding it firmly. When the dog can trot around the room and maybe jump over an 8-inch (20-cm) jump with the dumbbell in his mouth, try a front *sit*—using the food as a guide—to take the dumbbell. This will lay the foundation for correct fronts on the *retrieve* later.

When the dog can do nine "*Take it*" exercises on the move and hold the dumbbell for at least 10 feet (3 m) while moving, you are ready to progress to the next step.

1. Taking the dumbbell from the floor is on a par with getting the dog to take it while moving and continuing to move. These are the two hardest concepts for the dog to master in the retrieving exercise. Expect to take some time, be patient, and above all, do not use any force or show any negative reactions during this phase of training. Pick the hardest thing you ever learned and remember it. Hold that thought as the dog struggles through these learning experiences.

2. Go back to the "*Take it*" from a *sit* or *stand*, except make your dog reach down for the dumbbell. Do this in one-inch increments. Make sure the dog is having no problems with each level before going any further.

3. When you can get the dog's head to the floor, you will find he has no objections to picking up the dumbbell so long as you have at least one finger on it. But your dog may act as if he never heard of the exercise when you take your hand away. You just have to take your time and keep working. Tease the dog a little by moving the dumbbell out a little, then back; try to get your dog excited about what is happening. Eventually he will catch on.

4. Once the dog will pick up the dumbbell when it is on the floor and you are not touching it, place the dumbbell out a few feet at a time repeating the previous exercise until you can slide the dumbbell out 10 feet (3 m) and send the dog for it and get a positive response.

5. Next, try tossing the dumbbell a few feet out and doing the *send*. Keep using the "*Take it*" command and let the dog go get it as soon as he wants to.

From the time the dog gets the idea of picking the dumbbell up from the ground and bringing it back, you can incorporate a good *front* presentation. Use the food, just as you have been doing, to get that straight *front-sit* before you take the dumbbell—never use force. You do not have to do a *front* every time, but do them as often as possible. Eventually, the dog will chain going out, getting the dumbbell, returning quickly, and sitting straight in front as one exercise.

When the dog can do all of the above smoothly and correctly, move on to the next step, which is adding the command that will bond all of the required movements into the final exercise. From now on use the word "*Fetch*" just before the "*Take it*" command. (*Fetch* is a generic term. Any word will do, just pick one and remember exactly what it means and be consistent with its use. Some Schutzhund handlers use "*Bring*.") The only time you will use the "*Take it*" after this transfer has been made is when you have a problem or are teaching the dog to hold a new item. Having these training words is especially useful if you go to the directed glove *retrieve* or the metal dowel *retrieve* in AKC utility (advanced) competition. When the dog responds to the word "*Fetch*," drop the "*Take it*" command.

At this point in the training, you will be sending the dog almost at the same time you throw the dumbbell. The dog must go enthusiastically out and get the dumbbell and return it to you with a good straight *front sit* both on the flat and over a 12- to 14-inch (30- to 35-cm) jump before you try to put any control on the exercise at all. Later you will teach the dog to wait for the command before going, but not in the beginning.

Once the dog has mastered all of the retrieving skills needed to compete and has matured a little, you can start teaching him to wait for the command before going. The foundation work for this will have been laid earlier in the "*Find it—Here*" and in the section on "*go-outs*" where you

will slip a nylon cord through the dog's collar, throw the food out in front, but restrain the dog with the cord. At the same time you will say "*See it*," and show the food by pointing at it. As soon as the dog looks at the food, give the command "*Get it*" or "*Go*" and turn loose one end of the nylon string looped through the collar. The dog can then go directly out to get the food. Work on this until the dog will stand (or sit) with no tension on the cord and wait for the command before going.

As soon as the dog has mastered the concept of waiting for a command before going for the food, do the *setup* and throw the dumbbell. Make sure you restrain the dog for a second, then give the "*Fetch*" command and release. Repeat this exercise in sets of three until the dog will watch the dumbbell but wait until given the command before going after it. You can use the *chain-breaker* along with the slip cord to establish this sequence.

The use of the slip cord is especially helpful in polishing the retrieving and going away exercises in both Schutzhund- and AKC-type obedience competitions. It also lays a good foundation for polishing off-lead obedience training as the dog matures and you are getting ready for competition.

Jumps

Given the command of "*Jump*" or "*Over*" and presented with an obstacle, the dog is to jump the high jump or scale the scaling wall. Many handlers use a separate command for clearing an obstacle and another for scaling or climbing an obstacle. However, the separate commands seem to make little difference to the dog that has a tendency to jump those obstacles he has been taught to clear, if possible, and scale those that he has been taught to climb.

Review the exercises on jumping through the hoop in the chapter on puppy training. If you have not done so, add this to your dog's experience. It is an excellent foundation and will be extremely helpful.

Many excellent studies have been done concerning jumping and the effects it has on the dog. Most dogs seem to be able to jump with reasonable ease, and few end up any worse for wear if handlers observe a few commonsense rules. Young dogs may be started on jumping as

Improvised Jumps

Improvised jumps may be constructed from cardboard, plywood, a pull-down window shade secured to two uprights, a bed sheet over a bar, and any number of readily attainable materials. Plans for any of the jumps are readily available on the Internet. The hoop is a great way to warm up a dog. It is easy to transport and doesn't require any setting up. Kids love it and it offers one more diversion for therapy dogs.

early as eight weeks, if the 4- to 6-inch (no higher than 8 inch [20 cm]) (10- to 15-cm) board is used. However, it is unwise to attempt to put any dog (regardless of breed and willingness) over his adult jumping height before he is at least one year old. Therefore, plan to do all of your training and practice jumps between 8 inches (20 cm) and two-thirds of the dog's adult jumping height (the average is about 26 inches [66 cm] for German Shepherd Dogs and most Schutzhund–trained breeds). In Schutzhund competition, there is a written requirement that dogs be at least one year of age before they can compete due to a mandatory 39- to 40-inch (91- to 102-cm) jump for all dogs, regardless of breed, at each level of the Schutzhund competition.

AKC requires the dog to jump his height at the withers on the bar and solid and twice that number on the broad jump. Always check the newest regulations before entering any competition. Rules change over the years and vary among trial-holding groups.

The foundation for the jumping exercise is the *"Find it—Here"* exercise. If the dog will go out after the goodie and return on command, you are ready to start training the dog to jump on command. Set up a jump or simulated jump (strips of wood or cardboard propped between any two objects such as a doorway, two cans, or lower braces of chairs) on a good jumping surface such as a carpeted hall or outside on the ground. Inside is better with young puppies because a

surface on which the dog can see the food is essential in the beginning. If you are working with an older dog and want to work on concrete (garage, walk, or any smooth surface), you can buy a 3-foot (91-m) carpet runner 15- to 30-feet (4- to 9-m) long from the bargain bin at many carpet houses. This is much safer on the dog's "landing gear" as training progresses and also provides better traction.

Show the dog the food, toss it over the jump so that it lands a few feet out, and send the dog after it. Use "*Here*" to recall the dog back over the jump to the food reward. After the first one or two successful jumps, substitute the word ("*Over*" or "*Hop*") you are going to use for the *jump* command for "*Find it*." You can still use the informal "*Here*" for the

recall, but make sure the dog never comes back to you by going around the jump. If this occurs, go up to the jump and show the dog the food to get him back over the first time or two. If the dog tries to establish a pattern of coming around, take the food, catch his nose with it, and lead him back to the opposite side and over the jump before giving the food. It takes only a time or two for the dog to realize he is wasting time coming around. Most dogs quickly realize that to get the food, they have to go back to the other side and still come over the jump.

Letting the dog go on his own (as opposed to running with him on lead), allows the dog to approach the jump under his own control and gauge the speed and distance needed to clear

the obstacle. As the jump height is raised, this becomes increasingly important.

When you move outside or increase the height of the jump and start making the dog wait for the command before going over, you will switch from throwing the food to putting it on a coffee can several feet out from the jump before sending the dog. Never place it on the ground. You want the dog to be able to make a quick decision as to whether the food is there or not. This is not a guessing game where the dog is allowed to hunt for the food until it is found or he gives up. The food is either obviously there, or it isn't.

When it isn't, the dog goes to Plan B, which in this case will be to pick up the dumbbell and return over the jump for the reward. The dog needs three jumps (a set), no more than three times a day, at the practice levels. The dog needs enough practice to be moving confidently and accurately at the level for his age before adding the dumbbell to the routine.

When the dog is ready to carry the dumbbell and you have completed the jumping exercises above, let the dog jump the barrier with the dumbbell in his mouth a few times. When the dog is comfortable carrying the dumbbell over the jump at the current acceptable height, then you are ready to start the *retrieve* over the jump. Lower the jump to between 8 to 16 inches (20 to 41 cm) and teach the *retrieve* over the jump. Do it just as you are doing the *retrieve* on the flat. You may have to encourage the dog the first time or two, but most dogs flow into this with no problems at all. Gradually raise the level of the jump over a period of time, which must be regulated by the dog's maturity level, until the dog will retrieve the dumbbell over the correct competition height.

Practice should alternate with jumps to the food for exercise and *retrieves* with the dumbbell. You can run five or six practice jumps at the two-thirds height, but refrain from doing more than two or three each day at full competition heights. After the dog is reliable, only one full jump every two or three days is sufficient to stay ready for competition.

Fun Matches and CGC

It is not necessary to complete all of the training before starting to have fun with your dog. Informal obedience matches start at a much more relaxed level than sanctioned trials although you cannot earn legs toward titles. A leg consists of a qualifying score at a licensed trial. It takes three legs under three different judges to complete a title.

Before the novice level, matches offer a prenovice class. This includes all of the novice exercises performed

Agility weave poles.

is extremely informal when compared to sanctioned events. This is strictly a pass/fail event. Write the AKC or check online for complete rules. Many obedience classes use this as part of their graduation.

The AKC offers the Companion Dog (CD), Companion Dog Excellent, also called open competition (CDX), and the Utility Dog (UD) titles. Each level builds on the previous and adds additional skills.

on a 6-foot (1.8-m) lead. The *recall* is shorter as well as the distance you have to go away from the dog on the *long sit* and *down* exercise. You can enter both prenovice and novice on the same day. Entries are generally made at the match.

Many clubs offer the Canine Good Citizenship (CGC) test. While approved by the AKC, the execution

Additional Competitions

Dogs that have finished the UD are eligible to compete for the Utility Dog Excellent (UDX). The Obedience Trial Championship (OTCH) is based on a point system involving the placement of the dog and the number of dogs in competition.

There are many interesting obedience competitions sponsored by a variety of groups. The Internet is an excellent source of information. Contact your local obedience club as well as the GSDCA for additional information. The best way to find out what is going on is to get involved and start meeting other people who share your interests.

Walking the seesaw is an agility exercise that will help develop balance and confidence in your dog.

Chapter Nine

Conformation Training Toward a Championship

General Requirements

The German Shepherd Dog is one of the most beautiful dogs in motion. The smooth trotting gait that distinguishes him from all other breeds is demonstrated best in a large ring with secure footing such as grass, sod, or rubber matting.

All conformation or breed championships require that the dog accumulate 15 points with two of the wins being three or more points in one show (these are called majors). The majors must be won under two different judges. Five points are the maximum number of points a dog can win at any one show.

Points are earned based on the number of animals defeated. This involves a complicated system that causes point values to change from region to region. Current updated guidelines are available from the AKC.

Entries for dogs and bitches are separate but the classifications are the same. Dogs (in general refers to both sexes but to males only when discussing classes) from 6 to 9 months and 9 to 12 months are entered in puppy classes. Novice is for dogs that have not won points or three first places. American-bred is for dogs that were born in America (often used for dogs too old to be puppies and not mature enough to show in the open level). Bred-by-exhibitor entries must be shown by their breeders only. Open is for all other entries and is generally where the more mature animals are shown.

Dogs winning their class will return for the winner's class. Bitches (females) and dogs (males) are judged separately. Once the winner is selected, a reserve winner will be chosen in case, for some reason, the winner is later found to be ineligible.

Winners Dog and Winners Bitch will return to show against all finished champions (called specials) for Best of Breed. Best of Opposite Sex to Best of Breed, and Best of Winners (Dog or Bitch) are also chosen from this class. Point records and charts are available at the superintendent's desk at any dog show. These are very helpful in figuring out the more advanced point distribution.

A dog will never come away from a competition with fewer points than the highest pointed animal he defeated that day.

All Best of Breed winners return to compete for four Group placements at the end of the breed judging. The German Shepherd Dog competes in the Herding Group.

Winners of each group come back to compete for Best in Show.

If you plan to enter shows, you need to get on the mailing list for show premiums. These addresses are listed on the Internet at *AKC.org.* Indicate you are interested in conformation and German Shepherd Dog shows.

Obtain the AKC rulebooks for showing, record keeping, and discipline, and read them thoroughly. If you have any questions, either call, write, or visit the AKC Internet site. If you are going to play the game, it is essential to know and understand the rules.

Review the chapter on the standard. The AKC has an excellent video on the German Shepherd Dog that includes the standard, well illustrated, plus comments on different examples of the breed. The German Shepherd Dog Club of America (GSDCA) also furnishes a breed packet including an illustrated standard that is quite handy for reference.

Training for Conformation Showing

Conformation training for German Shepherd Dogs is best started with a puppy; however, older dogs can often be trained successfully. German Shepherd Dogs are shown and presented differently from most other breeds. The German Shepherd Dog is moved at a trot (a flying trot) around the ring in a counterclockwise fashion at a fairly brisk clip. Most handlers use an 8- to 10-foot (2.4–3-m) lead. This allows the dog to move out in front of the handler to show both the dog and the movement to better advantage. Dogs must be trained to go smoothly, turn corners, and stop correctly.

Conformation showing helps breeders select dogs that best represent the standard of the breed.

1. The *stop, stand*, and *stack* are trained with both placement and food (called bait). The dog is encouraged to stop in the *stack*. This is done with food, along with a helping hand. As the dog comes to a *stop*, catch the collar between the ears with the right hand. Slide the left hand down the dog's back to the dog's left hind leg, stopping it. The dog will generally move the inner (right) leg forward. Say "*Good stack*," give bait, and perform the *two-pat release*. Repeat until the dog does it automatically.

2. Work on front feet only if the dog is placing them incorrectly. Otherwise, leave them alone. Eventually you will want to be able to place all four feet where you want them and have the dog remain in position until released. Work on this gradually, one foot at a time.

3. While holding the collar between the ears with the right hand, move the left hand from the dog's shoulder blade down to the left front elbow. Pick up the elbow and place the foot where it should be, facing forward and under the shoulder.

4. Switch hands so you are holding the collar with the left hand and moving the right front elbow with the right hand. Move the left rear foot back by either reaching over the dog and placing it or reaching under the dog. The last foot to be moved is the dog's right, which you move forward to a position almost even with the center of the dog and slightly toward you for balance. The dog should be balanced and the left back hock should be perpendicular with the ground, never on a slant. The front feet should be straight under the dog and not at a lean either forward or backward.

5. Once the dog can be stacked and will hold a *stay*, move in front and use the bait to get the dog's attention.

6. Do not let the dog come to the bait; always take it to the dog. Some dogs can catch food and do an excellent job of catching tossed bait. Practice catching the food as a separate exercise.

Tossing the food in front of the dog will sometimes help to get an alert expression on the dog. This is fine, except never let the dog go to the food. Always either retrieve the bait and give it to the dog, or give him another piece then or later.

Teaching the dog to move out on the lead can be done in several ways. One person can work the lead and another can run in front of the dog, calling him. Give a command such as "*Go*" or "*Run*." Pick your own command. The reward will be getting to go to the person and getting a treat.

If you are working alone, you can start out using a target, but it is much harder to make the switch to free movement with no target. Young dogs tend to want to pull ahead on the lead because they are excited about everything. Take advantage of this tendency and connect it with a command. After the dog has a good grasp of moving out, teach the "*Easy*" command so he doesn't pull all of the time. The commands "*Easy*" and "*Let's go*" work well together.

Gaiting Patterns and Ring Procedures

The two major patterns for showing are going around the ring and down and back. If possible, watch the judge before your dog is scheduled to show. Most judges keep to the same pattern. After you pick up your arm band at ringside and secure it to your upper left arm, you will be called into the ring by the number on your armband. They will have you bring the dogs in and line them up. After a brief look, you will be ordered to go around the ring together. The first handler in line generally checks to see that the person next in line is ready before going. The judge will indicate where you are to stop. Handlers keep a distance of a few feet between the dogs so that the judge can walk completely around a dog.

After the initial gaiting, the judge will examine each dog individually and have that dog go away and come back in order to see if the dog is gaiting correctly. The dog will then make one or more complete circles of the ring and return to the end of the line.

When the judge has examined all of the dogs, they will be placed in order and the judge will indicate which dog is first, second, third, and

This class is lined up for the judge to get an overall impression. The dogs are stacked (set up in a show pose) with bait or by positioning.

fourth. Those dogs will line up in the ring in front of markers, show the judge their armbands, and receive their ribbons.

Second-place dogs should remain in the vicinity until after the judging of Winners. If the dog that went first is selected for Winners, the second-place dog in that class will go back in to compete with the other first-place dogs for reserve winners. Since Winners can come from any class, it is important to remember this.

Grooming

Start early getting the dog used to having his mouth opened and teeth examined. Go over the dog from head to tail. Check (gently touch) testicles often. Using the command "*Make Nice*" as the judge approaches often relaxes the dog and makes the exam less stressful. It also reduces the likelihood of the young dog deciding this is the moment to assert his budding guarding tendencies. As insurance, "*Make nice*" is a very valuable command.

In the conformation ring, you can offer food to the dog to settle him down. The dog can move some, but must accept the examination without resentment or aggression. The examination is more thorough than in obedience, as the judge is feeling the shoulder blade for placement, the ribs for construction, and the topline and hips for structure. The judge will also, very smoothly and gently, check to see if a male dog has both testi-cles. The teeth are also examined, but you have the option of showing them to the judge rather than having the judge open the dog's mouth.

When working with young dogs, use the command "*Teeth*" each time you look at the teeth. In the beginning, use your fingernail to scratch the canines as you are saying "*Teeth*." Then give a reward for compliance. As the training progresses, introduce the dog to the tooth scaler by gently touching the canines and then rewarding.

Eventually, the dog should let you clean his teeth whenever you want, which should be about once or twice a year. Dogs trained this way have no problems with the teeth examination in the conformation ring.

Since dogs must be thoroughly groomed prior to showing, this is another area that will have to be addressed. Training the dog to stand on the grooming table with the grooming lead on takes time. Start by placing the puppy or dog on the table. Pet, brush, and treat the dog the first time or two. Teach the dog to get on the table and stay until given the command to get off. As the dog comes off, hold the collar in the right hand and place the left arm under the dog's stomach to ease him off the table rather than letting him jump off. This will be especially helpful later if the conditions are crowded or the footing is uncertain.

Get the dog used to the dryer, spray cans of conditioner, and any other distractions he may encounter as part of his grooming routine. German Shepherd Dogs are bathed, blow-dried, and brushed prior to being presented in the ring. Getting the dog ready for the ring consists of making sure the nails are short, the teeth are free of tartar, and the coat healthy and clean.

During the shedding season, careful turning of the coat is advised. Moisten the coat; remove the dead undercoat gently with a metal comb or pin brush and blow dryer. Coat conditioner may be used to help prevent drying and split ends. Some groomers wet the dog down, then

blow dry shortly before going into the ring to give the dog a fresh look.

Never trim a whisker off your dog. German Shepherd Dogs are not trimmed, scissored, clipped, plucked, or in any way physically altered from their natural state. They are truly a wash-and-wear dog.

Double Handling (Historical Reasons)

Traditionally, that is the way this breed is shown in Germany and in German-type conformation shows (GSDCA-WDA) in America and throughout the world. German conformation shows often have a class gait for over an hour. Handlers inside the ring and doubles (often consisting of an entire family) will change often, as the people tire more readily than the dogs. They feel this gives the judge an opportunity to evaluate the dog's endurance as well as structure. A good idea, but hardly practical in most shows.

The exception, however, is in the specialties. Shows that are devoted entirely and exclusively to the breed generally have much larger rings and, due to the smaller number of entries, can allow the judging of a single class to go on for longer periods of time than would be practical at most breed shows. Best of Breed competition at the GSDCA National often goes on for hours. Conformation showing is an athletic sport for this breed and both dogs and handlers must be in excellent physical condition to successfully participate. Many exhibitors use professional handlers once they have passed the point where they are no longer physically able to present their dog. Others use handlers because there are a few dogs that simply will not show well with their owners. They are too attached, want to look at them constantly, and refuse to move out and away when in the ring.

Conditioning and Additional Training

Many exhibitors condition their dogs with bicycles, golf carts, jogging, and other forms of physical activities that build muscle and endurance. German Shepherd Dogs are excellent at play retrieving, swimming, agility, herding, and any number of sports that can be used to keep in top physical shape.

From the beginning of your training, work on *sits*, *stands*, *downs*, and *stays* as described in the puppy training section. Working these exercises off lead will enable you to pick up and expand on this training later without undue stress on you or the dog. The German Shepherd Dog is extremely intelligent and versatile. He will have little difficulty in distinguishing obedience type of work from conformation if you follow the OPT schedule. Many of today's champions are multiple-titled dogs that exhibit their genetic heritage and

bring pleasure to their owners. They are capable of learning through a variety of training techniques. The OPT is offered as one method specifically designed to combine the many versatile components of this particular breed.

All-Breed and Specialty Shows

All-breed shows are sponsored throughout the world by various organizations. The American Kennel Club (AKC) is the largest in America, with the United Kennel Club (UKC) being the second. Much smaller, but still presenting another excellent showcase for the breed is the States Kennel Club (SKC).

In addition to the all-breed shows, there are various types of specialty shows throughout the year. The

largest and most popular is the annual German Shepherd Dog Club of America (GSDCA) extravaganza. Five or six days of herding, obedience, tracking, agility, conformation, working dog competitions and programs all center on the one breed. The GSDCA also sponsors several Futurity and Maturity shows, which are not AKC point shows but are set up to give breeders an opportunity to showcase their best stock. Dogs must be nominated shortly after birth to be qualified to enter these shows.

German Shepherd Dog specialty shows are sanctioned by both the AKC and the GSDCA and sponsored by specialty clubs throughout the country. These shows are dedicated to German Shepherd Dogs only and often draw five-point majors from all across America. Often they have obe-

dience or temperament tests for German Shepherd Dogs and other breeds in conjunction with the shows.

The dogs at specialty shows should reflect the top breeding stock. These are the shows that attract the more serious breeders and exhibitors and the competition is often keen and exciting. There are generally more elaborate trophies than those given at most all-breed shows.

Specialty shows are much smaller overall than all-breed shows and often are held in areas adjacent to motels where it is easier to see the dogs out and about and socialize with the breeders and exhibitors. If you are looking for more information on the breed, this is an excellent place to go. Check the GSDCA Internet site or write the GSDCA for dates and locations.

Chapter Ten

Tracking

Tracking Events

The Optimum Placement Technique (OPT) offers a slightly different approach to training. This method is a quick and efficient way to teach the dog to track based on the assumption that you are interested in passing tracking tests and getting high scores on Schutzhund tracking.

The AKC Tracking Dog (TD) test is designed to measure the dog's ability to follow the trail and/or track a human, such as an escaped criminal or lost person, until either the subject is found or the trail is lost. Police dogs, on whose work the title was based, use both tracking and trailing techniques to locate quarry.

Neither the AKC nor the Canadian Kennel Club (CKC) tests are given numerical scores. Testing results are designated pass or fail, based on the dog's ability to stay reasonably close to a track and locate an article at the end. Getting off the track, overshooting or cutting corners, stopping for any reason, and any other diversions or digressions, although frowned upon, do not necessarily fail the dog if it demonstrates that he is following

the tracklayer, completes the track, and locates the article.

The Schutzhund tracking test is scored on the basis of a total of 100 possible points. Points are subtracted for such flaws as trailing (working the wind-carried scents and going wide of the track), overshooting the corners (a common problem with trailing dogs and wind direction), and handling errors generally associated with trying to keep the dog from getting too far off the track and from becoming tangled in the line when off course. Because of the points involved, tracking training should be somewhat different from that of a police dog upon which most training was based in the past.

In Schutzhund, the basic tracking exercise requires that the dog be able to follow a track within inches from start to finish, maintaining a steady pace and not overshooting or circling any corner. The track will never have been laid more recently than 20 minutes and can be up to four or five hours old, depending on the level of Schutzhund work the dog is pursuing. The dog is required to find and announce to the handler in a positive manner the location of two to several articles on the track as well as one at the end of the track.

Tracking Versus Trailing

Since this would seem to be the most efficient method of obtaining titles, training will be approached from a scoring point of view. With OPT training, the dog can get all of the AKC or CKC titles and still be ready to go on to Schutzhund without the necessity of retraining.

Most training methods date back to the original police training and consist of various ways of getting the dog to follow a track that has just been laid. While these are called tracks, they are in reality trails, since the trailing scent overpowers any beginning track scent that might be there for at least the first 45 minutes of most tracks. Most training methods begin with these unaged tracks and remain with them for the first few weeks of training.

What happens with this type of training is that the dog is being put on a track that is at its peak scent power for trailing and at its weakest scent power for tracking. For at least two or three weeks, the dog is run repeatedly on hot trails and cold tracks. Then, gradually, the dog is given aged tracks and the handler attempts to teach it to follow these instead of the previously taught trails.

This particular method is excellent for police and service dogs and will work with most dogs for AKC and CKC competitions. It allows the dog to add to his store of available resources (the trail scent) the ability to track and follow a person. This type of training, however, is extremely confusing to the dog that is intended

to be used only as a competition tracker. With this type of training, the dog is given a set of responses that you must later waste time demonstrating that you no longer want. With some dogs you may have to spend months teaching him not to do something (trailing) you just spent the previous three weeks teaching him to do. Obviously, this negative training leads to many really unnecessary frustrations and even more unnecessary hours of additional instruction.

So, in order to avoid wasted time and effort and to cut your training time by two-thirds of that generally needed to make a dog "track sure," let's concentrate on teaching only that part of the exercise you really want the dog to know—namely, how to track.

Tracking

Plan about an hour a day for about four or five weeks or an equivalent time period. You can do other things while the tracks are aging, but the actual laying and running will take some time. In the advanced stages you will need two or three hours once or twice a week.

There are a few basic items to mention. Never scold or correct your dog when training. Weather is not a criterion as to whether or not you will track. Tracks must be worked in all forms of weather.

It will help the dog internalize the training if you crate your dog at least 20 minutes to an hour before and

after tracking in the beginning weeks. Give the dog an opportunity to potty before starting the track. After the dog is working well, you can release the dog to more pleasurable activities after the track, if that is desirable or practical.

The hour of day you track is entirely up to you. Competition tracks are run from before daylight to after dark, depending on the circumstances. When it is a little cool and the grass has some moisture on it, either from dew or light rain, you will get the maximum benefit from your training. These conditions are particularly good in the early stages of the training when you would like for things to move along nicely. Later, once the dog learns the basics, you will need to work all types of terrain and in all kinds of weather in order for the dog to become widely experienced in the art of tracking. The more practice the dog gets under a variety of conditions, the less likely he will be to encounter a condition at the trial with which he will be unable to cope.

By now the dog should be accustomed to the process of using food to learn new exercises. Place a leather item, such as a 4-inch (10-cm) square cut from an old purse or shoe, or a glove on the floor or ground. Show it to the dog by using the food to lead his nose down to the article. Pick up the item, show it to the dog, and give the food reward. Repeat this exercise in sets of three until the dog will lie down easily when you motion with your hand from his nose to the article. (This exercise is easy if preceded by the nose-drop *down* in obedience.) Once the dog will go down to the article when you point, while the dog is still down, pick the article up and drop the food in the spot where the article was. As the dog is eating the food, say "*Good.*" When this has been worked to the point where the dog can do it easily, you are ready to lay tracks.

1. Find a spot of grass or plowed dirt big enough to lay about 20 to 50 paces of track. Put a tracking flag in the ground to your left as you stand facing in the direction you intend to walk.

2. Walk, not scuff or stomp, a good 2-foot (61-m) square to the right of the flag. This square of walked track is called a scent pad. Take about one minute to do this each time.

3. Drop an article on this pad and walk, taking very short, close steps, about ten paces out and make another scent pad about 1 foot (30 m) square and put an article in the middle of it.

4. Continue on until you have laid about three scent pads. At the end you may want to set a flag so you know the direction when you start. There will be no flag at the end of a regulation track, but flags are very useful in knowing where you walked your track during training.

5. At the end of the last scent pad, after you have placed the article in the middle of it as you did with the others, take a giant step forward, then leave the area.

You will now have some free time. Do not run any track in the beginning that has not aged 45 minutes to one hour. Actually, a track that has aged an hour or an hour and a half is better. This is the key to opening the lock faster. After about 45 minutes, most of the human trailing scent has begun to disperse and the track scent is becoming hot. A track that is an hour old is even better, as the track scent has, as a general rule, gotten slightly hotter (easier to smell) than the trailing scent by that time. You don't want to get it too old in the beginning, as you do want just a bit of the trailing scent to be present so the dog can learn to distinguish a human track from one of a car tire or an animal.

You may lay three or more of these short tracks or scent paths a day in the beginning, either one after the other or at different times during the day. During your entire training program lay tracks at all hours of the day and evening and in as many different types of weather conditions as possible. Let the dog learn all of this as he goes along.

After an appropriate wait, bring the dog out and tell him you are going to "do a little tracking" as you approach the starting flag. Put the 4- to 6-foot (1.2-m) lead on the dead ring of the plastic snap collar, since this is the training equipment most often used. If the dog is really a strong puller, you may have to go back and teach the dog to give to the collar (walk on a loose lead). It is really better to train the dog to go on a loose lead prior to starting your tracking training in order to avoid confusion and possible negative training. Go quietly to the scent pad and do a nose-drop *down* on the first article. Pick up the article and drop the food in the center of the scent pad. As the dog is sniffing the food and eating it, say "*Good track*" a time or two. If you are clever and hold the food in the bend of your little finger, you can drop it as you pick up the glove with the rest of your fingers and the dog will never figure out where the food came from.

As soon as the food is eaten, point to the track and gently lead the dog down it to the next scent pad and article. You can encourage the dog with little phrases such as "*Let's find another.*" As soon as you reach the article, do a nose-drop *down* and drop the food as you pick up the article. As the dog is eating the food, repeat "*Good track.*" Continue this praise and reward system to the end of the track. When you reach the last article, do the nose-drop *down*, pick up the article, drop the food in the scent pad, and let the dog eat it as you repeat "*Good track.*" Then, since this is the last article and the end of the track, reach over and give the dog two (remember, not one or six—just two) firm pats on his left side (*two-pat release*). Do this when you reach the last article of each track every time. You may say something like, "*That's it!*" or "*We're through*" if you want, but the two pats will come to mean to the dog that he has reached the final article and that, at least for right now, he is through

tracking. This will keep your dog from quitting too soon or from trying to continue on with the track after the last article in hopes of just one more reward.

Length of Track

The length of tracks the first week will correspond to your physical ability to run them. Athletic trainers can run a 30- to 40-yard track after the first two or three days. Those with bad backs or who are short of wind need to run several 20- to 30-pace tracks. The first week is the hardest, since you must point and direct the dog from one article to the next. After that, the track will be done with you standing up, except at drops, when you give the reward and retrieve the articles. While running the first week of tracks, stay close to the dog's right side and use a short lead held close to the collar for maximum control.

Tracking Goals by Weeks

First week: The goal of the first week is not to track, but rather to get the dog to go along as directed to articles that are immediately traded for something desirable. The dog will also be pairing the track scent (the scent pad under the article) with the food reward and the praise "*Good track.*" Your intention is to show the dog what you expect and let him discover the reward following a correct performance.

During the second week, the dog will begin to focus on the fact that the track (not trail) scent always goes between and connects the rewards, and that this scent is distinctive and different from the adjacent terrain. It is at this point that the older tracks are especially important, for they have almost no human scent left so the dog can associate the track scent with the interval between treats.

Never double-lay the beginning tracks. In advanced tracking tests, the dog must determine the direction of the track at the start, and dogs trained in the beginning with double-laid tracks have been taught that it doesn't make any difference which way the track goes as long as the dog follows it. This type of training will lead to failures in future events or long delays in retraining sessions.

Second week: During the second week you can also begin to introduce gradual turns, roads, changes of ground cover, or any other variation you wish. Keep the tracks short, so that the dog is still interested in the reward at the end. The length of the track you use will vary from dog to dog. Some dogs can go 300 to 400 yards the second week, while another may be going only 30 to 40 feet (9 to 12 m). Some dogs have lower enthusiasm levels, and their adaptation to distance must be gradually built up over a period of time. Other dogs will bound out ready to track for long periods of time by the second week. Evaluate your dog and train accordingly. It is also advisable to start letting other people lay some of your tracks at this time. Do this as often as possible during each successive week of training to help the dog become

accustomed to various tracklayers. Different weights in tracklayers produce different tracks.

Third week: In the third week, continue the 45-minute to two-hour-old tracks. Increase the dog's endurance for distance and difficulty of terrain and add turns as the dog is able to handle them. Slow curves, gradually tightened over a several-day period, seem to work better than abrupt right-angle turns in the beginning. Avoid areas in which it will be difficult for you to locate your track. You must know every step of that track. Take short steps, use soft earth, take advantage of the early morning dew (because you can see where you walked), use drops that are fairly close together, and/or use tracking flags or ties. Do whatever is necessary to allow you to know exactly where every step of that scent path is during those first few weeks.

In order to prevent the dog from going from flag to flag by sight, pick your area and place ten or more flags at random. Number them. When you lay your tracks indicate which numbers you are using each time. This will cause the dog to ignore flags because there is no pattern he can learn. Since there is no pattern, the dog will consider the flags like trees or grass.

If the dog appears to be following the sight of the articles, you can try several ploys. One consists of using very small articles and slightly covering them with grass. Another involves laying your track in grass high enough to hide the articles. You will also be putting greater distances between each article, thus making it more difficult for the dog to stay on the track and still try to use his eyes.

Fourth week: By the fourth week, begin to allow the dog to go out to the end of a 6-foot (1.8-m) lead. If the dog exhibits uncertainty, go back to using the shorter lead. If by the fourth week the dog is doing regulation-length tracks, then gradually extend the length of the lead over the next two weeks until the dog is at the end of the 32-foot, 9 inches (10 m) lead. If problems develop in any part of the tracking exercise, go back to the shorter lead to instill confidence, and stay with it until the problem is corrected. Check rules of desired competition to determine exact length of tracking leads as they vary some across organizations. Also determine type of harness required for the competition desired and start introducing it in the fourth or fifth week.

Every time you change ground cover and/or age of the track, a dog may have some minor problems until his experience includes nearly every circumstance that might be encountered. By now you have probably realized why food cannot be used on the track. The aging process affords all of nature's little wild ones ample time to spirit treats away, as well as making spoiled food a danger (in a hot summer sun many foods can quickly become toxic). The food scent on the track could also become such a distraction that it would slow the dog in learning the track scent. The dog would then have to unlearn the track-

Two-Pat Release

Keep in mind the *two-pat release* you give your dog at the end of each track. This is easy to forget in the beginning, so remind yourself until it becomes a habit.

ing of food before he could learn to track humans. Dogs have a very keen scenting discrimination ability; you do not have to walk with hot dogs on your feet to teach the dog to track. And unless you can talk the trial tracklayer into cooperating with you, this is really just time wasted. The bottom line is that eventually the dog must follow the scent made by the footsteps of a stranger.

As the dog becomes more expert at moving from one article to another, remove every other article from the track. Then reduce the number of scent pads placed around each article until only the first, middle, and last articles have scent pads. Next, remove the article from the starting scent pad and reduce the number of articles to the appropriate number for the level of AKC or Schutzhund training you are working at. Finally, occasionally do not give the treat on any of the articles until you have picked up the last one and walked off the field.

Experience has indicated that it is best to run at least one or two tracks a week with many rewards, one or two with only one treat at each of the required drops, one with the reward at the end, and one with the treat given off the field after the last article. Mix these runs up so that the dog cannot establish a pattern. This form of variable reinforcement leads to the most consistent performance over the widest period of time. Continue to use the word "*Good*," pairing it with food to make it a strong reinforcer for the dog even in the absence of the food. Occasionally leave a large knucklebone waiting at the last article and allow the dog to lie right down and have a really big reward. You can give the *two-pat release* on the spot.

Use your imagination and be creative with your tracking. Your dog will stay alert and always be anticipating something interesting along the track. Vary the types of articles you use from practical household items such as a flashlight to small objects such as empty bullet shell cases or crumpled business cards. Use wood, leather, metal, and plastic from time to time—you never know when someone will throw you a curve. At one Schutzhund competition, they used a rolled-up leather lead as one article and a wooden dumbbell about 3 inches (7 cm) long on a key ring as another. Many of the dogs missed the key ring. One conservation-sensitive handler passed by picking up a crushed drink can her dog sniffed at during an advanced Schutzhund track. It turned out that was one of the articles. That's another good reason to have the dog *down* to indicate that this really is an important find.

Use as many different tracklayers as is possible over the course of the

Rewards

Keep some empty 35-millimeter film containers handy if you want to use some treats on the track now and then. Use food that won't spoil. The dog will know the food is in the can. All you will need to do is open the container for him to get the reward. Use this sparingly and only with dogs that are not doing well with the regular program.

training. Use both men and women of varying weights and have them wear a variety of different footgear. Leather, rubber, and tennis shoes are most commonly favored with track-layers.

Once the dog is tracking full-length tracks at one hour old, then you must start working some fresher tracks into your routines until the dog can stay on the track when it is only 20 to 40 minutes old. These are extremely hard for the tracking dog as the trailing scent is very fresh, and the dog would much rather pursue the hotter scent than stay with the fainter and more difficult track scent.

Alternate between the fresher tracks and tracks aged up to two or three hours. Take several days with each new age change and go back to the one-hour tracks every so often to refresh the dog. Any time you make any change in the track age, start with the shorter tracks and build up to the longer ones over several days, depending on the ability of your dog.

Road Crossings

When you start road crossings, look for worn animal trails and paths in the meadows. Lay the tracks across them and help the dog until he adjusts to the change in smell. Next, go to safe and secluded lanes or roads. Many dogs will simply cross to the other side, pick up the track, and continue. They have learned that the track always goes straight across roads and paths. Next, find some paved surfaces and work these into your practice sessions. Park walks with grass on either side are excellent. When the dog is comfortable with a sidewalk, try for a safe concrete roadway. You should never work your dog on asphalt or macadam surfaces in hot weather. The oils, tars, and other components that constitute these surfaces, plus the oil and other debris spilled on them, can make these roads extremely damaging to your dog's sensitive nose. Most dogs need about 15 minutes to get their scenting ability back after trying to track across a regular blacktop (macadam, asphalt) road when it is hot. In order to train your dog to cross these surfaces should you encounter them in a trial, teach the dog to raise his head, go across the road, and cast for the track on the other side. This is the safest way to do this, and though you may lose a few points for this behavior, your dog will be able to immediately pick up the track on the other side and complete the course, a much more desirable alternative to possible failure.

Cross tracks can be introduced at any time during training. If you plan to lay your own cross tracks, you might want to carry a 5-gallon (19-L) paint can (full) in each hand. The extra weight will change the character of the track to some degree. Lay cross tracks the day before, as this will help the dog distinguish between the tracks accidentally laid down by the judge and tracklayers as they plotted the tracks the day before the trial. Occasionally dogs will pick up these cross tracks and follow them if they have not had previous experience dealing with them.

Lay cross tracks 30 minutes to an hour (when you are running two-hour tracks) after you laid the original track. This is one exercise where you really need another tracklayer. As you prepare for competition, occasionally have one person lay the track and another the cross track. If the dog ever tries to commit to one of the cross tracks, say *"Phooey,"* and direct him back to the correct track. It is a good idea to have a scent pad with the article a few feet past the cross so the dog can get an immediate reward for the correct choice.

In your training process, be smooth, be patient, and above all be certain you are providing enough time for you and your dog to master the basic technique of working together. This training method will not produce a frantic animal that drags the handler across country, but a steady working dog with a good understanding of the task expected and with the skill and determination to complete it.

The practicality of the OPT lies in its total flexibility, the segmented training that allows for extremely short working sessions to be effective, and the lack of stress for both dog and handler. Over the years this method has been found to produce learning that is long lasting, easy to polish, even after extended periods of disuse, and extremely enjoyable to both handler and dog.

Interesting Things to Know About Tracking

Scent patterns are to the dog's nose what color patterns are to the artist's eyes. Picture a meadow laced with millions of ribbons in an almost infinite number of different colors and hues. An artist could be given the end of one color pattern and could walk along following that pattern, even as it crossed and threaded through all of the others. Some people would have a problem where the colors came together and the hues and tints were very close to each other. Some would have a problem even distinguishing between the various shades of one color, and others would not be able to do it at all. This is the way the dog deals with the scent patterns.

Age

There is one other factor to consider when discussing scent that is unlike a consideration of color, and that is the element of age. Color patterns remain fairly constant, but scent patterns do not. Scent patterns do change in character as they age, until after an indefinite period of time they disappear. The dog must learn not only the identity of a scent at the time it was put down but also to identify it as the aging process operates to change it. This is why it takes time to train a dog to identify a human-laid track at the many stages of deterioration along with the changes that the ground is undergoing at the same time.

With controlled practice, the dog will develop this skill to an acceptable level. The length of time, number of tracks, and natural ability of the particular dog will all affect the dog's performance. All singers cannot hit high C, regardless of the amount of practice or the skill of their teacher. Part of what the animal brings to that tracking field was established long before you arrived on the scene, even if you were the dog's breeder.

There will always be some human scent, especially the skin rafts that hold the body scent so well, on any track encountered in the normal course of training. The effects of the wind, weather, and temperature will also influence the dog's behavior on the track. Under optimum conditions, a well-trained dog will put his nose down on the starting pad and not take it up until he has reached the end. Practice until the dog will stay right on the track for corners and through any change in ground cover despite any outside influences such as wind or distractions. However, optimum conditions rarely prevail, and each dog will bring to the tracking field certain traits and learned behavior that will frequently result in less-than-perfect scores.

Recording

When you track, keep a notebook handy so you can record various ground cover and weather conditions, the time of year and day, along with your dog's reactions. This will allow you to more accurately evaluate and predict your dog's behavior. Draw a map of each track and record the dog's reactions as accurately as possible. Sometimes previously unnoticed patterns in the dog's tracking skills (or lack of them) will show up when viewed over a period of time.

Excellent examples are found in the AKC tracking rulebook. These can be ordered direct from the AKC or picked up at many dog shows at the superintendent's desk.

Water

Always carry water for your dog. If it is hot, carry a canteen on the track in case the dog needs it. Also, never bathe your dog the day before or the day of the track. Shampoos, rinses, dips, sunscreens, and many other chemicals can cause the dog to "lose nose" for a period of time. Towel the dog down with water if needed for "freshening" and use sunscreen and insect repellent sparingly. Experiment during advanced training to determine what your dog can and cannot tolerate. The value of keeping records cannot be overemphasized.

Do not smoke around the dog, especially in the car. This can ruin a good dog's nose. It may also give him cancer.

Many medicines will inhibit a dog's capacity to do scent work. Avoid new medication prior to competition. Keep a detailed record of medications and unusual experiences the dog might have had at any time that could have any bearing on his tracking ability. This type of journal can provide valuable information about your dog's strengths and weaknesses. Refer to it often.

Title Requirements

Requirements and rules for various tracking titles can be obtained from the AKC and other organizations that host tracking trials. Addresses can be found in Appendix A of this handbook and online.

Most competition tracks run from 100 to over 1,000 yards with a varying number of articles to be indicated. Variances include cross tracks and change in ground cover, length, and age of the track.

The AKC is currently in the process of adding several new tracking titles as well as making some minor revisions to the tracking rules. These will be announced on their Web site in the future.

The OPT video on tracking offers excellent suggestions and examples at the starting levels of tracking. Once the dog has obtained his foundations skills, there are many excellent tracking challenges offered through competition or service activities. Each track is a unique experience offering challenges for both you and your dog. This activity can create a wonderful working relationship between you and the dog. As your communication skills develop you will come to appreciate the problem-solving potential of your dog. Dogs appear to approach tracking much the same way people go after crossword puzzles, working out each little section as they go. It is one activity that once they get into, they appear to enjoy for its own rewards. You also see this in herding and Schutzhund protection work where the performance is self-rewarding for the dog.

Chapter Eleven
Schutzhund

Meaning

Literally translated, Schutzhund means "protection dog." Actually, it symbolizes a great deal more. To a knowledgeable trainer, the word describes a dog that has been trained in tracking, obedience, and protection (sometimes called man-work or bite work). The dog must perform reliably and safely the necessary exercises to find a person, bark an alert to the handler, and hold the person, using whatever force is necessary, until support comes. Further, the term denotes a dog that will *let go (out)* on command, a dog controllable on or off lead in solitude or in a crowd, a dog that will perform even under the frequently terrifying racket of gunfire. In sum, the Schutzhund dog displays obedience, patience, courage, and control, ready to be released in the service of his owner to guard, to protect, or simply to please.

Schutzhund is not synonymous with police or attack training. The Schutzhund dog is a highly trained, versatile dog with exceptional discrimination in his biting habits. These dogs are not trained to attack on command, as are police dogs, but to react to a variety of situations in several select ways. The dog does not attack unless he senses a threat to the handler or to himself. Once the bite has been taken, the dog holds fast until ordered to *let go (out)* or until the victim stops struggling and stands still. His obedience and tracking are far above that expected of the average dog; however, most Schutzhund dogs are not as extensively trained in tracking as are working police dogs. A competent home obedience and personal protection dog can be safely trained in about 6 to 12 weeks. It generally takes at least two years to completely train and exhibit a dog to a Schutzhund III title.

Schutzhund as a Sport

As a sport, Schutzhund training and competition has taken hold in America in the past few years. The sport, which originated in Germany and spread across Europe, is finding a dedicated following among those dog people who appreciate the performance of a working dog fulfilling the purpose for which it was bred. There have been some stormy growth years in the Schutzhund movement in America, as different groups sought to be the principal sponsor or representative of the sport. Currently, there are three major groups (with new ones forming at a rather steady rate) that hold trials, license judges, and grant titles in America. Most use the standard VDH rules as adopted by the West German National Kennel Club, with occasional minor adjustments.

The American Kennel Club offers a Working Dog program. Check the *AKC.org* site for details. The German Shepherd Dog Club of America offers AKC trials at their yearly National.

When you start training, at whatever age the dog happens to be, you need to take inventory of your dog's strong points and also the area(s) in which he needs improvement. A good trainer and a caring, humane owner must recognize that some dogs simply do not have the temperament to stand up under the stress of training and gunfire. They may have the temperament, but lack the physical ability to do the necessary jumping and fighting that are required for Schutzhund. A 40-inch (1-m) jump is difficult for some dogs and impossible for others. The push or drive needed when the dog does the protection bite work takes excellent neck and jaw muscles, good teeth with a proper bite, and a strong rear to hold the dog as he moves either forward or backward when biting the sleeve. Be realistic when you are evaluating your dog. He might be the most loving, beautiful companion you have ever had, but still not be suitable for the extended physical training program necessary to produce a Schutzhund dog.

There are only eight obedience exercises that a dog needs to know in order to gain all three Schutzhund titles. Most of these are covered in the puppy training and obedience chapters. These exercises are combined in a variety of different ways at the various levels, but there still remain eight specific commands that the dog must be able to execute from a variety of positions and under different stresses and stimuli. For the tracking section, there is only one new exercise the dog must learn. In the protection phase, there are only two commands and three exercises that are required knowledge for the

A Schutzhund dog will bite and hold on to the sleeve.

When the dog attacks, it is expected to retain its bite until told to release by the handler.

The dog is expected to release on command and guard the decoy.

dog beyond what he has been taught from the earlier chapters.

Almost any dog can perform the above requirements under optimum conditions and limited variations. It is only through success at increasingly altered and changed positions, order, and combinations of the known exercises that the dog and handler determine whether they have achieved the goals toward which all training aims. Those goals are to produce, first, a dog that knows a command so well that he will execute it regardless of the circumstances or situations under which it is issued, and second, a trainer who is capable of bringing the dog to that level.

A standard current VDH and AKC Working Dog trial rule book should be obtained to help clarify the location of the various exercises in the

trainer's mind. There are minor variations in some exercises from one level to the next and almost no change in others. Still other exercises are introduced for the first time in advanced title levels, and some are dropped from one level to the next. The sequence of teaching the exercises is less important to the training than to the actual performance, which is under the direction of the handler. Stated another way, it does not matter to the dog whether there are changes from one level to the next, since the training is intended to result in an attitude rather than a sequence of unrelated steps.

Assuming that your dog has the mental and physical makeup necessary for learning and performing and that you have achieved the required level of training, you may wish to

The scaling wall is very similar for both Schutzhund and agility, except that in Schutzhund the dog retrieves a dumbbell on the return.

secure a score book for your dog. You can obtain the names of those Schutzhund clubs sponsoring trials and ask to be placed on their mailing list for trial and seminar notices.

A good way of keeping up with the various club schedules is to subscribe to the national publication for each group. Useful addresses and clubs are listed in Appendix A of this book. You should already have obtained a copy of the current VDH Schutzhund and AKC Working Dog rulebook in order to be thoroughly informed about updated regulations, since these do change from time to time. All of the American Schutzhund organizations and most European ones use the VDH rules. Get a current copy and study it before attempting to put all of your exercises together. Learn the sequences and always be alert to the fact that rules are subject to interpretation by different judges.

For more information on Schutzhund visit the German Shepherd Dog Club of America Working Dog Association Web site. They also post information on current rules and upcoming events.

compete in a trial sponsored by one of several Schutzhund organizations. In many, but not all, of the organizations, it is necessary to join, obtain a membership card, and

Chapter Twelve
Herding

Bred to Herd

The German Shepherd Dog was first and foremost a herding dog although it has been underutilized as such in America. However, with the current interest in the AKC herding program, breeders are doing much more testing to identify those German Shepherd Dogs that have retained interest in stock beyond simply chasing.

While testing for the remnants of natural herding instincts in order to utilize those dogs in today's breeding programs, breeders are also looking for dogs able to be trained for the protection routines of the standard Schutzhund tests.

Today's dogs that still retain remnants of their original talents are rapidly taking a predominant role in many breeding programs. In addition, testing of progeny for herding potential and ability, along with the desire to protect, coupled with the ongoing search for a sound body, could eventually help revitalize the breed.

The aspects of herding, such as nurturing and protecting, are the most valuable of all qualities in a good home or protection dog. Many have found that breeding only for protection and obedience or only for conformation leads to a watered-down version of what was once a truly great dog.

Instinct Tests

With the advent of the AKC herding program, the opportunities for exposure, learning, and training to titles have expanded rapidly across the country. Many herding breed clubs are now offering Herding Instinct Tests as well as full competition and title events at both the national and regional levels. Courses include fetching, driving, and tending at three levels: Beginning, Intermediate, and Advanced. In addition to the AKC, the American Herding Breeds Association (AHBA) offers a variety of tests and trials throughout the United States.

Most instinct tests will be conducted in a small pen with the dog on lead. Any type of stock (sheep, goats, cattle, or ducks) so long as it is dog broke is suitable. Dog broke stock is any stock that is accus-

tomed to being worked by dogs. At least one qualified instructor must be present. It is unnecessary for the dog to chase the stock or for the handlers to chase or strike the dog during this test. The dog is started on lead. Generally, the instructor holds the lead so the dog can be correctly controlled and evaluated. It is often desirable, but not always necessary, to have the owner in the pen with the dog and stock.

The dog is evaluated on his desire to interact with the stock. Once the dog's level has been determined, the owner decides on the next step in the training program. Many breeders are content with an HIC (Herding Instinct Certificate) that would indicate, if trained, the dog would be an acceptable herding dog. However, if they feel that their dog can progress to become an acceptable herding dog either for home use or competition, then the next step is deciding on which course they will train for and how they will proceed with their training. It is advisable to select a trainer who is familiar with both the herding and tending aspects of the German Shepherd Dog. The AKC and the American Herding Breeds Association (AHBA), as well as the Australian Shepherd Club of America (ASCA) and many Border Collie groups offer many tests and trials in herding. The AKC, specific tending organizations, and Schutzhund groups offer tending trials. The Internet is an excellent source for contacts.

Herding as a Way of Life

While much of herding tends to focus on competition, there are still many situations in which the dogs may be used for daily help around the farm. Never fail to give the dog a chance to use his skills to help you out. It could make life easier and more enjoyable for both of you.

The qualities that make a superior guard dog with the discrimination to be gentle with children, small dogs, and puppies, are inherent in the working herd dog. Shepherd means to guard, herd, nurture, and protect. Failure to retain the herding heritage of the German Shepherd Dog will eventually lead to a dog that in many ways lacks the outstanding versatility and the combination of courage and ferocity with gentleness and devotion that made the original German Shepherd Dog the ideal of so many dog lovers throughout the world.

Appendix A

Addresses

American Kennel Club Web site
www.akc.org
Gives access to all registration concerns, show superintendents, upcoming shows for all venues, health information, information on all AKC-sponsored events both conformation and all performance, and many other helpful and useful areas of interest to both the companion dog owner and potential exhibitor.

Corporate Headquarters
(212) 696-8200
AKC
260 Madison Avenue
New York, NY 10016

AKC
Operations (registrations)
(919) 233-9767
AKC
5580 Centerview Drive
Raleigh, NC 27606

German Shepherd Dog Web site
www.gsdca.org/show includes results information, information on handlers, organization, calendar of events, communication, stud dogs, brood bitches, miscellaneous, other

organizations, how to become a member, standards, dogs for sale, puppies, and more.

German Shepherd Dog Club
of America
www.gsdca.org
http://www.gsdca.org/gsdca_joomla/ index.php

**German Shepherd Dog Club
of America—Working Dog**
Association Web site
www.gsdca-wda.org
Gives information on training, licensed clubs, Schutzhund and Working Dog competitions, and much more.

Canine Videos and Training
**OPT Obedience/Performance/
Conformation Training and
Educational Materials**
OPT Obedience/Tracking/
Schutzhund tapes or DVDs/
Lesson Plans keyed to German
Shepherd Dog Handbook
229 Glendhenmere Lane
Hazel, KY 42049
(270) 436-2858
E-mail: maryba@toast.net
Web site: *glendhenmere.com*

To get on dog show mailing lists and get additional information on all dog show superintendents go to *www.akc.org/events/conformation/superintendents.cfm.*

Superintendents serve various areas of the United States; superintendents for performance events are often listed separately. When on the events page, look up the various performance areas you are interested in and check out those superintendents. Kennel clubs are good sources of information about local dog shows and performance events. Clubs near you can be found on *AKC.org* Web site.

Superintendents can also be found in *Dog World* magazine available at your local stores or on the Internet.

Schutzhund Organizations in America

German Shepherd Dog Club of America-Working Dog Association (GSDCA-WDA): The Schutzhund Organization of the German Shep-

herd Dog Club of America offers competitions to purebred German Shepherd Dogs that are members of the German Shepherd Dog Club of America. It operates under DVG rules. The organization sends German Shepherd Dog teams to Germany and elsewhere in Europe to compete in International Competitions and Championships. The official magazine is the *WDA Newsletter.*

Unless you speak and read German, you will need a current English translation of the rules for your use. The rules are changed occasionally; therefore, it is necessary to maintain an update on any rule book that you may have. Any person wishing to become involved in the competitive aspects of Schutzhund or the Working Dog sport in America should obtain a current translation from the club or group of interest.

The American Kennel Club currently sanctions Working Dog trials. Check *AKC.org* for rules, trials, and related information.

Appendix B

Bibliography

All of the following were written by Dr. Mary Belle Brazil-Adelman

Dog Training Book: Vol. I (1982). (includes: The Australian Cattle Dog: History, Selection and Training). Murray, KY: Creative Printers.

A selection of articles from 1977 through 1984 published in *Off-Lead, Dog Sports*, and *Creative Printers* dealing with various aspects of obedience, puppy raising, Schutzhund, herding, and tracking.

Dog Training Book: Vol. II. (1984). Murray, KY: Creative Printers.

A selection of articles from 1980 through 1984 published in *Dog Sports, Off-Lead, German Shepherd Quarterly*, and the Question/Answer column from *Paris Post-Intelligencer* and the *Murray Ledger* and *Times* newspapers on protection, tracking, herding, problem solving, and obedience using food and the OPT method.

Dog Training Book: Vol. III. (1995). Hazel, KY: Canine Printing.

A selection of articles from 1983 through 1995 published in *Front and Finish, Australian Cattle Dog Annual, German Shepherd Quarterly, German Shepherd Review, AKC Gazette, The German Shepherd Book, American*

Careers, Dog Sports, and *Off-Lead* on obedience, herding, careers in dogs, tracking, and problem solving. Includes the breed column for *AKC Gazette*.

Dog Training Book: Vol. IV. (1995). Hazel, KY: Canine Printing. A selection of articles from 1983 through 1989 published in *Paris Post-Intelligencer* on herding, general dog information, and problem solving.

Dog Training Book: Vol. V. (1995). Hazel, KY: Canine Printing. A selection of articles from 1983 through 2000 in *Australian Cattle Dog Annual, The Standard: Companion Animal News, Paris Post-Intelligencer,* and *German Shepherd Quarterly* on general problems, health, and obedience.

Adelman, Mary B., Kent Allen, and Anne Moss. (1988). "Animal Trainers." Chronicle Guidance Brief #508. Morovia, NY: Chronicle Guidance Publications, Inc.

Adelman, Mary B., S. Mueller, W. Davis, D. Arner, and J. Elliott. (1988). "Dog Trainers." Chronicle Guidance Brief #574. Morovia, NY: Chronicle Guidance Publications, Inc. Also, picture cover for "Dog Trainers."

Appendix C
Related Reading

Barwig, Susan, (ed.). (1986). *The German Shepherd Book*. Wheat Ridge, CO: Hoflin Publishing Ltd.

Barwig, Susan, and Stewart Hilliard. (1991). *Schutzhund*. New York: Howell Book House.

Battaglia, Carmelo. (1998). *The Proper Care of German Shepherds*. TFH Publications.

Belfield, Wendell, and Martin Zucker. (1981). *How To Have a Healthier Dog*. San Jose, CA: Orthomolecular Specialties.

Coren, Stanley. (2003). *How to Speak Dog*: *Mastering the Art of Dog-Human Communication*. New York: Free Press.

(1995). *The Intelligence of Dogs*. New York: Free Press.

Fogle, Bruce. (May 1999). *Dog Breed Handbooks: German Shepherd*. DK Publishing.

Hulse, Capt. G.L. (1973). *New Techniques in Canine Training and Development*. Australia: Wentworth Books.

Lanting, Fred. (1990). *Canine Hip Dysplasia and Other Orthopedic Problems*. Loveland, Co: Alpine Pub.

____. (1990). *The Total German Shepherd Dog*. Loveland, Co: Alpine Pub.

Lyon, McDowell. (1966). *The Dog in Action*. New York: Howell Book House.

Onstott, Kyle. (1977). *The New Art of Breeding Better Dogs*. New York: Howell Book House.

Scott, John, and John Fuller. (1965). *Dog Behavior: The Genetic Basis*. University of Chicago Press.

Stephanitz, Capt. Max von. (1950). *The German Shepherd Dog*. Germany: Himmer KG. (copy available from Wheat Ridge, CO: Hoflin Publishing Ltd.)

____. (1925-reprint 1982). *The German Shepherd Dog in Word and Picture*. Arvada, CO: Hoflin Publishing Ltd.

Syrotuck, William G. (1972). *Scent and the Scenting Dog*. Westmoreland, NY: Arner Publications.

Tossuti, Hans. (1942). *Companion Dog Training*. New York: Howell Book House.

Titles and Other Abbreviations

The following are some of the more common abbreviated titles and/or ratings.

Conformation Ratings

American

Basically the championship indicates that this animal is a fairly good to superb representation of the breed as described in the standard and has no disqualifying faults. It also implies a certain level of trainability and social skills because the dog must work close to other dogs and handlers and accept examination by the judge who, in most cases, is a stranger to the dog.

Championships are also awarded by a number of other groups, few of which carry the value of the AKC. This is primarily due to the rigorous requirements for becoming an AKC judge as opposed to the casualness with which many of the other groups select judges. Most other groups also have far less stringent require-

ments to attain the championship.

Canadian champions (Can. Ch) require only that the dog acquire ten points. No majors are required.

United Kennel Club (UKC) (U-Ch) and States Kennel Club (SKC) (S-Ch) also offer fairly structured shows that are similar in many ways to the AKC but not as stringent in their requirements of the number of dogs that must be defeated to become champions.

The FCI is an international association of dozens of national and breed clubs. It awards the CACIB, loosely translated as International Champion. The AKC is not at present a member club so AKC–certified pedigrees would not contain this information.

The GSDCA presents the AOE (Award of Excellence) to champions that received a Select rating at a GSDCA National Specialty show, have OFA–certified hips and elbows, have passed the GSDCA Temperament Test, and have at least one additional performance degree. Performance includes obedience, tracking, herding, agility, and/or a

Schutzhund title. Since its inception in 1990, among the many that have received the AOE, seven have been Grand Victors or Victrixes (the top winning German Shepherd Dog at the National Specialty).

The ROM (Register of Merit) is earned by the specific animal for the production of several champions plus 100 points earned by its progeny in both conformation and performance events.

The GSDCA also sponsors the TC (Temperament Test), which checks out the dog's willingness to be approached by strangers and encounter unusual sights and sounds (including gunfire), as well as his reaction to a hostile person.

Health certifications include the OFA (Orthopedic Foundation for Animals), H (indicates normal hips), and EL (indicates normal elbows). A Canine Eye Registration Foundation (CERF) number indicates normal eyes. A cardiovascular examination report filled out by a certified veterinarian ACVIM (Cardiology) and a T3 and T4 thyroid test (done by an endocrinologist through any veterinary service) are among the more extensive tests done by many serious breeders.

Performance

The list of performance titles is extensive and the German Shepherd Dog can compete well in obedience, rally, tracking, agility, working dog trials, and herding. List of possible degrees or titles, rules for obtaining them, shows, and areas of interest may be found at *AKC.org*.

There are many other organizations sponsoring various titles available in America and many foreign countries. Your best and most current source is the Internet.

Index